Recipes

FOR A GOOD TIME

Recipes

FOR A GOOD TIME

ELVIS ABRAHANOWICZ
BEN MILGATE

MURDOCH BOOKS

DEDICATION

People have come to know us as the face of our restaurants but Joe Valore is our other partner. He's the guy behind the scenes — the one person who's had unwavering faith in us from the beginning. Joe gave us the opportunity and the confidence to open the restaurants at a time when no one else was taking us seriously.

Bodega, Porteño and Gardel's Bar wouldn't be standing without him because we can only do what we know how to do, and that's cook. Joe keeps these machines well oiled and running; he's always the first to come in and the last to leave, but he gets the least amount of recognition.

You won't see many pictures of him as you look through the book because he doesn't need, or want, the attention. We dedicate this book to you, Joe. Our story only exists because you help us create it.

CONTENTS

FOREWORD

Many moons ago, my girl and I staggered into this newish food hall called Bodega. We grabbed two seats at the bar in front of the exposed kitchen. As we came to our senses we realised this cool new eatery was playing familiar music. It was The Black Keys' *Rubber Factory* album. Good sh*t.

Next, we raised our eyes to see two well-tattooed young men massaging the bits that became the dishes for the people. Interesting looking cats. Really focused and moving with style as they dished it out and shook the shaker for a dish ready to go. We started getting some of those dishes, and getting grand advice and offerings of liquid accompaniments. We got to know those two boys behind the counter. Soon enough, the lady with the stunning hair, mind and body came into the fold, as did the awareness that something very special was going on here. We left feeling full and fine, and thinking we had found a new long-time hang.

Seven years down the track and Bodega and the super house of Porteño and Gardel's Bar are Sydney institutions. Not institutions of stuffiness and attitude, but institutions of amazing, consistent food, booze and service. It's the personal touches from Ben, Elvis, Sarah and Joe that make a meal an event and a night to remember. It's like we wandered into a fancy, home-style, awesome food party. I reckon that's what these recipes will do — bring a lil' bit of Porteño and Bodega and the boys' magic touches into your own home. Tastes good.

BT (food lover)

INTRODUCTION

From the moment Ben Milgate, Elvis Abrahanowicz and Joe Valore opened the doors to their first restaurant — an unapologetically loud-and-louche tapas bar serving Spanish and South American fare in the worst bit of Surry Hills, under a cloud of rock 'n' roll they had Sydney wrapped around their heavily inked pinkies.

Ben and Elvis set about dishing out the kind of food they wanted to cook, the way they wanted to serve it, in a restaurant they wanted to eat in, flipping the bird to crisp white tablecloths and easy listening. While Sarah (Elvis's now wife) flitted around the room chatting at a thousand miles an hour, curls perfectly intact, no matter how many plates she was running. The whole thing was, and still is, mesmerising.

Hit Bodega and you'll see off-duty bands, on-duty rockabillies with quiffs and sets standing proud, and just about every food fan in the city either propping up the bar, squashed in the tiny room dancing elbow to elbow, or queuing up outside to get in for a taste. The lines haven't gotten any shorter since they opened in 2006. If anything, the food has just become more delicious.

You can almost see the evolution of the restaurant marked out on the chefs themselves. Over the years they've swapped shag 'dos for quiffs, miso-cured salmon for salt cod pancakes and The Cure for The Black Keys. They've just about run out of room for any more tattoos, but the ideas keep coming.

Then again, it's not just Porteño's whole beasts cooked over a giant ring of fire in the middle of the restaurant or Justin Townes Earle playing a secret gig at the bar upstairs that makes their restaurants so special. It's not even those fish fingers at Bodega.

What sets them apart is the family they've created around them: the sommeliers across both restaurants (who also run everything behind the scenes) Joe Valore and Rachael (Sarah's sister), Elvis's parents, Hilda and Adan, who literally keep the kitchen fires burning every morning and stay up until the wee hours rolling empanadas the night before. And there's not a single member of this extended family who doesn't love it.

In some ways it's not what the fellas do that makes their restaurants so special, it's what they don't do. If Ben and Elvis are both cooking together, just watch them for five minutes. They barely exchange a word. They're like dancers who know exactly what the other's move will be before they do it themselves — albeit dancers who look like they're on weekend release. The thing is, they make it all look so effortless and easy.

They want you to feel like a friend who's dropped by for a snack and something to drink. They'll never make you feel stupid for picking up the cutlery the wrong way, or putting your carefully pickled veal tongue into a bread roll and eating it like a sandwich. They want you elbows deep in good times.

This book is essentially a face-first dive into the extraordinary lives of the Valore–Doyle–Abrahanowicz–Milgates. Welcome to the family.

Myffy Rigby

BEN MILGATE BY ELVIS ABRAHANOWICZ

Ben and I became friends as soon as we started working together. We'd both been travelling in Argentina, so we had that in common, and Ben had just had his first big tattoo done — the sleeve on his right arm. The first thing you have to know about Ben is that he has an amazing work ethic. It doesn't matter what's going on or what's happened, the work always gets done. He always pushes through it. The only days Ben's ever had off work were when his children, Clementine and Frankie, were born.

He's also a really caring guy. His most important rule is to always look after your friends. He started living on his own when he was sixteen. Both of his parents were separated and had moved to the US, so he had to learn to cook for himself. He used to tell me stories about one of his stepmums who would serve Spam that had been seasoned thickly with oregano and then baked in a toaster oven. I think one of the reasons he became such a great chef was because of that (even though he still loves Spam). That, and the fact that he was going to get kicked out of school anyway. Ever since we became friends we've always spent Christmas with my family. My parents love him.

We've been frustrated with each other over the years at times, but we've never been angry with each other. I think one of the most important things is that we never say no to an idea. Working side by side with someone the way we work can be pretty hard. You can't get away from them so you have to be really open. We see each other every day. Even though now we're both working separately across the two restaurants, we still pick each other up from work and talk about the day. There have even been a few Christmases where we've unintentionally bought each other the same gifts.

Then there was the time we both separately bought Guitar Hero on the same day and sent each other photos of ourselves playing the game in our undies. That was a bit weird.

ELVIS ABRAHANOWICZ BY BEN MILGATE

Our lives have really changed in the past nine years. When I met Elvis in 2004 I was single and doing some crazy stuff. In the years since then we've opened our first restaurant together, we both got married, I had two kids, we opened another restaurant. A lot's changed. In the last few years we've really grown up together and have an incredibly strong, brother-like bond.

You might not know this about Elvis, but he's a little bit shy with strangers. Once he gets going though, he talks so much rubbish and you can't stop him. He's also really creative and his plating-up skills are amazing. We kinda have the same palate and we bounce ideas off each other. He's got a big heart, too. He always wants to be sure everyone around him is doing all right. For instance, he'll drop me off at home and wait till I open the door before he drives off.

The longest Elvis and I have spent without hanging out was when he and Sarah went to South America without me. It was just a couple of weeks, but I didn't know what to do. I ended up compiling a huge list of movies I'd never seen, watching them all day and just walking around the city. I'd never want to run a restaurant without Elvis. One day, I'd love to open something in Nashville, but I'd never do it without my best friend.

Cooking-wise, I think Elvis draws a lot from the way he's grown up, and even from what his dad ate growing up. Those family stories . . . I don't have that sort of thing in my life. His family and my family are polar opposites. He sees his folks every day. I haven't talked to my old man in five years. When I first met Elvis and Sarah, my parents were both overseas so I was a bit of an orphan. At Christmas, I would go to their houses and they'd look after me. Elvis's father is like a second dad to me. He's taught me more about cooking with fire than any other chef I've worked with, as well as all sorts of other things. He's 62 and he just blows my mind. The man is amazing.

Did I mention Elvis can skull a can of beer and smoke a cigarette at the same time? It's a hell of a party trick.

Bodega

The idea for Bodega came from the two of us being sick of working in fine-dining restaurants. We'd just left a meeting with the chef we were both working for at the time, thinking, 'Let's open our own place.' So we called Sarah and asked her how to get a loan. She said, 'Why the hell do you want to try and get a loan? You can't even get a credit card.' That's when we called Elvis's brother-in-law, Joe, who decided he wanted to take a chance and give us an opportunity.

We walked the streets for three months looking for a site. We'd both quit our jobs and we were all living together in a tiny flat in Redfern with Sarah working three jobs to support us. We'd meet with people every day, but they'd take one look at us and go, 'Pfft . . . nup.' There was one meeting in Rushcutters Bay where we'd been out all night the night before for Elvis's birthday, and we turned up to the meeting on the Sunday morning, reeking of booze. We got in there and the lady, after grilling us about what we wanted to do with the place, said, 'So, what you're telling me is you want to turn my hard work into some psychedelic rock 'n' roll café? No, no, no.' We walked out. The site is still vacant.

We ended up getting a phone call from the guy who owns the current site on Commonwealth Street, and he offered us a deal we couldn't refuse. We just opened the kind of restaurant we'd like to go to: somewhere with great quality food in a fun environment. There was nothing like it in Sydney at the time. There was nowhere you could go that played good music, where you could sit at the bar and watch the chefs work.

From the moment we opened the doors in 2006 the whole thing has been a gamble. We didn't know what was going to happen, we just did it. And it turned out to be the best thing we've ever done.

Fish Fingers

SERVES 8 (2 FINGERS PER PERSON)

This is our signature dish. It'll never ever come off the menu. We eat one every day. You've got to eat them straight away with your fingers. We don't call these fish fingers because they're fingers of fish, we call them fish fingers because you've gotta use your mitts. Some people try and use a knife and fork and we go 'Oi! What are you doing? Use your hands!' This is the recipe for our classic kingfish fingers, but you can make any variation you like: mackerel, raw scallop, pickled veal tongue, crab, even Spam. But do you know what it's really all about? The garlic toast. Fresh, raw seafood on burnt, charred toast is really delicious. It's the contrast of the toast — all warm, salty and charred — with the clean, cold fish that makes this so incredible.

4 cuttlefish

4 slices levain bread (crusty
   semi-sourdough), about
   1.5 cm (⁵/₈ inch) thick

2 garlic cloves, halved

extra virgin olive oil

river salt flakes

2 × 250 g (9 oz) pieces of sashimi-
   grade hiramasa kingfish top loin,
   skin off and pinboned

2 teaspoons chopped coriander
   (cilantro) leaves

2 tablespoons fresh lime juice

¼ of a small brown onion,
   thinly sliced

freshly ground white pepper

1 small piece of mojama,
   about 2.5 cm (1 inch)
   (see Glossary)

To prepare the cuttlefish, gently pull off the tentacles so the insides come out with them. Cut just underneath the eyes and remove and discard any beak from the tentacles. Save the tentacles to fry up later, as a snack. Discard the eyes and any insides and gently pull the cartilage from the body and discard. Remove the skin, wash gently then dice.

Preheat a large grill plate or barbecue grill over a high heat and grill the bread until well charred on both sides. Rub the hottest side of each slice of bread with half a garlic clove then drizzle heavily with extra virgin olive oil and season with salt.

Cut each slice of bread into four equal 'fingers'.

Slice the kingfish 5 mm (¼ inch) thick and place on the toast.

Mix the diced cuttlefish in a bowl with the coriander, lime juice, some salt and a drizzle of olive oil.

Place a spoonful on each piece of fish then top with a couple of very thin slices of onion and season lightly with white pepper.

Microplane the mojama liberally over all of the fingers and serve.

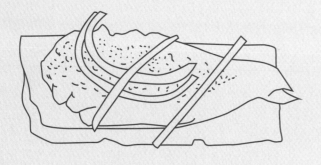

**GARLIC TOAST
SASHIMI KINGFISH, CUTTLEFISH CEVICHE
SHAVED MOJAMA & RAW ONION**

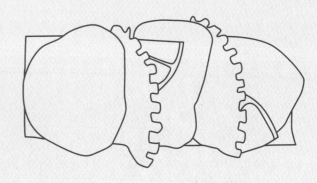

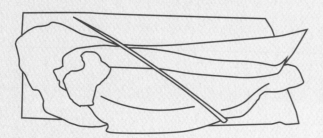

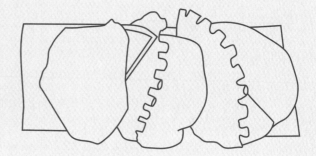

**GARLIC TOAST
RAW SCALLOP
PICKLED OCTOPUS & LIME**

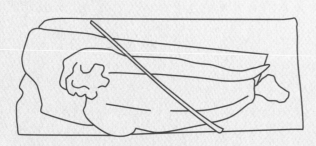

**GARLIC TOAST
SCORCHED BONITO, SEA URCHIN
CHIPOTLE MAYONNAISE & CHIVE**

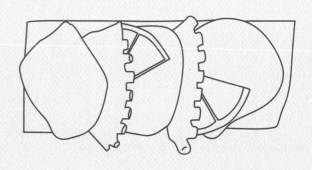

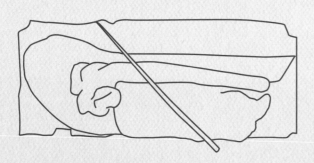

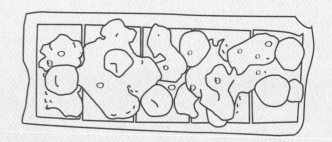

GARLIC & CITRUS TOAST
SMOKED SALMON, AVOCADO
& PICKLED JALAPEÑO

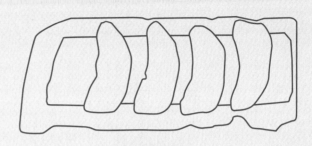

GARLIC TOAST
TUNA BELLY
& SLICED BOTTARGA

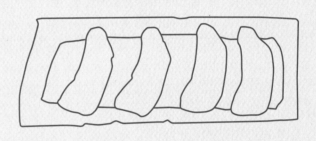

GARLIC TOAST
GRILLED SPAM
CHILLI MUD CRAB
& SALSA GOLF

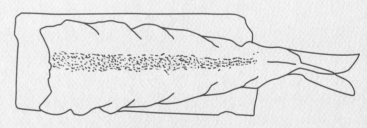

GARLIC TOAST
MANZANILLA & LIME
MARINATED PRAWN
& SEAWEED SPRINKLE

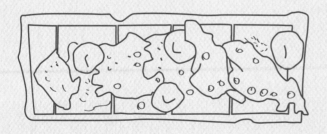

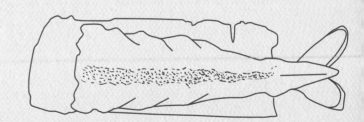

Morcilla-Stuffed Calamari

with Pickled Green Tomatoes

SERVES 8

4 × 150 g (5½ oz) morcilla sausages
8 Hawkesbury River squid, each
    approx. 15–20 cm (6–8 inches) long
200 ml (7 fl oz) extra virgin olive oil
4 pickled green tomatoes (see pg 278),
    thinly sliced
55 ml (1¾ fl oz) pickling liquor (from
    the pickled green tomatoes)
2 tablespoons finely chopped
    preserved lemon (see pg 279)
4 red bird's eye chillies, very
    finely chopped

Preheat the oven to 120°C (235°F/Gas ½).

Peel the morcilla, cut them into small pieces and place on a baking tray in the oven for about 5 minutes, or until soft and pliable.

Scoop the morcilla into a piping (icing) bag and set aside in a warm place.

To prepare the calamari, gently pull off the tentacles so the insides come out with them. Reserve the ink sac. Cut just underneath the eyes and set aside the tentacles. Remove and discard any beak from the tentacles. Discard the eyes and any insides and gently remove and discard any cartilage from the body. Wash the calamari gently.

Make a small incision in the calamari, just before the tip of the pointed end. Gently pipe the morcilla into the body so it's just over half full (take care not to overfill them). Place the tentacles in the open end, lightly press down on the calamari and seal the end with a toothpick.

Preheat a grill pan over a high heat. Empty the ink sacs into a bowl, add half of the extra virgin olive oil and lightly mix together. Coat the stuffed calamari in the ink oil then transfer to the hot grill.

Cook for 2 minutes on all sides, starting with the flap side down, this will set the shape. Let them rest for 2 minutes after cooking, then remove the toothpicks and slice.

Place slices of the pickled tomatoes on a plate or sharing platter and then arrange the calamari pieces on top or to the side.

Make a simple, quick vinaigrette dressing with the remaining oil, pickling liquor, preserved lemon and chilli. Dress the plate and serve.

Morcilla & Scallops

with Braised Cabbage, Tahini Sandwich & Pickled Cauliflower

SERVES 8

TAHINI SANDWICH

1 sheet of brik (brick) pastry
  (see Glossary)
cottonseed oil for frying, plus extra
100 g (3½ oz) basic mayo (see pg 274)
2 tablespoons hulled tahini paste
1 tablespoon plain yoghurt
fine sea salt

CABBAGE

¼ small savoy cabbage, ribs
  removed, leaves separated
1 tablespoon olive oil
1 garlic clove, crushed
50 g (1¾ oz) unsalted butter, diced

MORCILLA & SCALLOPS

1 × 150 g (5½ oz) morcilla sausage,
  sliced into 8, skin removed
8 scallops
olive oil

TO SERVE

1 handful of finely grated cauliflower
1 tablespoon thinly sliced spring
  onion (scallion)
1 tablespoon finely chopped chives
2 sprigs of coriander (cilantro),
  finely chopped
ginger pickle (see pgs 31–32)
fish sauce
extra virgin olive oil

Preheat the oven to 200°C (400°F/Gas 6).

TAHINI SANDWICH

Cut the brik pastry into four rectangles the length of four scallops side by side.

Fill a medium heavy-based deep saucepan a third full of cottonseed oil (no more) and heat to 165°C (329°F).

Deep-fry the pastry pieces, one at a time, for about a minute, or until golden all over, then drain on paper towel.

Mix the mayo, tahini and yoghurt in a bowl, season to taste then place into a piping (icing) bag.

CABBAGE

Heat a large dry saucepan over a high heat, add the cabbage and lightly toss until very slightly coloured. Add the olive oil, garlic and a splash of water and cover to steam lightly. Turn down to a medium heat.

Steam for about 5 minutes, stirring occasionally until just tender, then stir through the butter.

MORCILLA & SCALLOPS

Place the morcilla slices on a baking tray in the oven for 1–2 minutes to warm through.

Preheat a medium frying pan over a medium–high heat, drizzle the scallops with olive oil and cook them for 1 minute, or until golden then turn them over, leave for 30 seconds then remove from the pan.

Pipe some tahini mayo on a rectangle of the pastry then top with another piece of pastry, creating a sort of sandwich.

Mix the cauliflower, spring onion, chives and coriander together and season with a few spoonfuls of ginger pickle.

Place four scallops in a line on a plate and top each one with a slice of warmed morcilla. Spoon some of the cabbage around the plate and season with a few drops of fish sauce and a drizzle of extra virgin olive oil.

Balance the pastry sandwich on top of the morcilla and top with some cauliflower. Repeat with the remaining ingredients and serve immediately.

Pork Belly

with Braised Silverbeet, Raw Clams & Sherry Ramen Sauce

SERVES 8

1.2 kg (2 lb 10 oz) pork belly,
   bone in and skin on
200 g (7 oz) coarse rock salt

BASE STOCK
2 kg (4 lb 8 oz) pork bones
2 pig's trotters
6 spring onions (scallions)
1 brown onion, halved
a large knob of ginger,
   roughly chopped

SHERRY RAMEN
1 large onion, thinly sliced
a knob of ginger, sliced
40 ml (1¼ fl oz) vegetable oil
250 ml (9 fl oz) Oloroso sherry
2 tablespoons white miso paste

SILVERBEET
1 kg (2 lb 4 oz/1 bunch)
   silverbeet (Swiss chard)
1 garlic clove, minced
1 red bird's eye chilli, sliced
60 ml (2 fl oz) extra virgin
   olive oil

TO SERVE
24 New Zealand surf clams
   (vongole)
80 ml (2½ fl oz) extra virgin
   olive oil
20 ml (½ fl oz) fresh lime juice
fine sea salt
freshly ground white pepper
2 radishes, thinly sliced
1 small white onion,
   thinly sliced

PORK BELLY

Get a non-reactive tray large enough to fit the pork belly whole, and sprinkle half the salt evenly around the tray.

Place the belly in the tray, skin side down, then rub the remaining salt into the bone side of the belly. Leave in the fridge for 24 hours.

The next day, wipe off the excess salt with a paper towel. Place the pork in a large steamer and steam over a medium–high heat for 3–3½ hours, ensuring that the water is topped up every now and then.

When you can stick a skewer into the meat easily, it's ready. Remove from the steamer, leave to cool to room temperature then cover with plastic wrap. Refrigerate overnight.

BASE STOCK

Put 1 kg (2 lb 4 oz) of the pork bones and one trotter in a pressure cooker, cover with water, then throw in the spring onions, onion and ginger. Close and lock the lid of the pressure cooker and place over a high heat. When it reaches pressure, reduce the heat to low and cook for 20–25 minutes. Follow the manufacturer's instructions for releasing the pressure and opening the lid, then strain and discard the bones, onion and ginger.

Return the stock to the clean pressure cooker. Add the remaining bones and trotter and top up with enough water to cover everything. Repeat the cooking process, then strain and discard the bones.

SHERRY RAMEN

Sweat the onion and ginger in a very large saucepan over a low heat with the vegetable oil until the onion is very soft.

Add the Oloroso sherry and reduce down over a medium heat until there is almost nothing left. Add all of the base stock and the miso paste then reduce to a sauce consistency. Strain and discard the onion and ginger.

SILVERBEET

Trim away the white stems of the silverbeet, leaving two large pieces of leaf. Heat a large dry saucepan over a high heat, add the silverbeet leaves and a splash of water then cover to steam lightly over a medium heat until soft and breaking down.

Take the lid off then add the garlic, chilli and extra virgin olive oil and fry, stirring occasionally, until really well cooked.

TO SERVE

Shuck the clams (saving any of their juices) and place 1 tablespoon of the juices in a bowl with the extra virgin olive oil, lime juice and a pinch of salt and pepper. Add the clams to the bowl and toss to coat.

When ready to serve, trim away the rib bones from the pork, cut in half lengthways and then slice into 5–7 mm (¼ inch) thick pieces. Lightly oil and salt the sliced pork then reheat it, either by steaming it again or grilling it lightly.

Lay the silverbeet on plates, top with slices of pork belly then dress with the clams, radish and onion, and drizzle over the sherry ramen.

Corn Tamales

with Mushroom Pibil & Mole Verde

SERVES 8

PIBIL (SEE NOTE)

1 brown onion, diced
3 garlic cloves, chopped
2 red bullhorn capsicums
(peppers), diced
150 ml (5 fl oz) olive oil
5 drained piquillo peppers
(approx. 110 g/3¾ oz)
1 × 220 g (7¾ oz) tin of chipotle
peppers in adobo sauce
1 teaspoon annatto seeds,
finely ground
200 g (7 oz) oyster mushrooms,
sliced
200 g (7 oz) shiitake
mushrooms, sliced
300 ml (10½ fl oz) freshly
squeezed orange juice
sherry vinegar
fine sea salt

MOLE VERDE

2 brown onions, thinly sliced
6 garlic cloves, crushed
a small knob of ginger, peeled
100 ml (3½ fl oz) blended oil
(95% canola + 5% extra
virgin)
1 × 600 g (1 lb 5 oz) tin of
tomatillos in brine, drained
fine sea salt
200 ml (7 fl oz) water
1 teaspoon cumin seeds,
toasted and ground
6 cloves, ground
100 g (3½ oz) pepitas
(pumpkin seeds)
90 g (3¼ oz) coriander
(cilantro) stems and roots,
roughly chopped

CORN TAMALES

4 corn cobs
50 g (1¾ oz) margarine
75 g (2¾ oz) grated fontina
cheese
300 g (10½ oz) fine semolina
½ teaspoon fine sea salt
½ teaspoon caster (superfine)
sugar
¼ teaspoon baking powder
5 large banana leaves

TO SERVE

400 g (14 oz) crème fraîche
½ teaspoon black sesame seeds
4 spring onions (scallions),
sliced
40 g (1½ oz) pepitas (pumpkin
seeds)
a few sprigs of coriander
(cilantro), leaves picked
1 lime, cut into wedges

NOTE: THIS MAKES MORE THAN
YOU NEED BUT IT'S ALSO GREAT
ON TOP OF SCRAMBLED EGG
TACOS FOR BREAKFAST.

PIBIL

Sweat the onion, garlic and the bullhorn capsicum down in olive oil in a medium saucepan over a low heat until very tender.

Meanwhile, blitz the piquillo peppers, chipotle and ground annatto seeds in a blender.

Add the mushrooms to the saucepan and cook down for 30 minutes, or until softened. Add the orange juice and reduce for a further 30 minutes, or until emulsified and thick.

Stir in the blitzed pepper mixture and cook for a further 30 minutes, stirring frequently.

Add a splash of sherry vinegar and salt to taste. Set aside to cool.

MOLE VERDE

In a medium saucepan over a very low heat, slowly sweat the onion, garlic and ginger in the oil for 25–30 minutes, or until the onion is really tender, but not coloured.

Add the tomatillo, salt to taste and water. Simmer for a further 40 minutes, then allow to cool to room temperature.

Put the tomatillo mix, cumin, cloves and pepitas into a blender and blitz to a smooth paste. Add all of the coriander and blend for 2–3 minutes, or until smooth and pourable.

Check the seasoning then put in squeeze bottles and use at room temperature.

CORN TAMALES

These need to be prepared at the last minute, so when you've got everything ready to go, make the filling. Use a large sharp knife to remove the kernels of corn from the cobs then blitz the kernels in a blender with just enough water to get it moving.

Melt the margarine in a small saucepan over a low heat.

Put all the ingredients, except the banana leaves, in a large bowl and mix together until well combined.

Trim the banana leaves into ten 30 cm (12 inch) squares. Lightly grill the trimmed leaves, one at a time, to soften them, then place each one on a large piece of plastic wrap. Put a few large spoonfuls of corn mix in the centre of each leaf and add a tablespoon of pibil.

Fold the leaf over to enclose the mix and wrap each tamale in the plastic wrap. Steam in a large steamer basket over a saucepan of boiling water, topping up the water in the pan every now and then to make sure it doesn't boil dry. After 40 minutes, unwrap one of the tamales, it should be cooked through. If not, steam for another 10-20 minutes and check again.

TO SERVE

Serve the tamales with the mole verde, crème fraîche, sesame seeds, spring onions, pepitas and coriander over the top, and wedges of lime for squeezing over.

Smoked Brisket

with Fried Eggs, Onion Rings & Barbecue Sauce

SERVES 8

1.2 kg (2 lb 11 oz) piece of smoked
   wagyu brisket (see pgs 130–133)

OLD BAY BROTH
500 ml (17 fl oz) reduced animal stock
   (see pg 270)
1 teaspoon Old Bay seasoning
   (see Glossary)
fine sea salt

ONION RINGS
150 g (5½ oz) plain (all-purpose) flour
¾ teaspoon dried yeast
300 ml (10½ fl oz) beer
cottonseed oil, for deep-frying
2 white onions, sliced into 3–4 mm
   (¼ inch) rounds

TO SERVE
8 eggs
chipotle mayo (see pg 274)
barbecue sauce (see pg 272)
4 spring onions (scallions),
   thinly sliced

OLD BAY BROTH
Bring the animal stock to the boil in a small saucepan over
a high heat. Add the Old Bay seasoning and a pinch or two
of salt, to taste. Whisk, then strain the broth, return to the
pan and put over a low heat to keep warm.

ONION RINGS
Place the flour and yeast in a bowl. Add the beer and whisk
to combine. Leave in a warm place for 15 minutes, or until
bubbly and active.

When ready to serve, fill a medium heavy-based saucepan
a third full with oil (no more) and heat it to 180°C (350°F).

Dip the onion rings in the batter and place in the oil. Cook
in batches for 2–3 minutes, or until light golden. Remove with
a slotted spoon and drain on paper towel.

TO SERVE
Warm the serving plates in a low oven while you fry the eggs in
two large non-stick frying pans with a little oil.

Carve the brisket into 5 mm (¼ inch) thick slices (two per
person) and place onto the warmed plates.

Pour over some of the hot Old Bay broth, top with a fried egg
and some onion rings, then drizzle over some chipotle mayo and
barbecue sauce. Scatter some spring onion on top and serve.

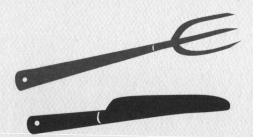

Arepas
with Black Bean Sofrito & Fresh Cheese

SERVES 8

BLACK BEAN SOFRITO
100 g (3½ oz) dried black turtle
  beans (see Glossary)
fine sea salt
1 brown onion
3 red bullhorn capsicums
  (peppers)
1 long red chilli
2 red bird's eye chillies
3 garlic cloves
125 ml (4 fl oz) extra virgin
  olive oil
200 g (7 oz) drained piquillo
  peppers
2 teaspoons smoked paprika
55 ml (1¾ fl oz) sherry vinegar

CORN PICO (SEE NOTES)
2 corn cobs, husks on
1 small red onion, finely
  chopped
2 tomatoes, deseeded and
  diced
3 sprigs of coriander (cilantro),
  leaves and stems finely
  chopped
1 green jalapeño, finely diced
juice of 1–2 limes
extra virgin olive oil

**NOTES: THE CORN PICO CAN
BE MADE UP TO FOUR HOURS
BEFORE SERVING.
QUESO FRESCO IS AVAILABLE
FROM SPECIALIST DELIS
AND SUPPLIERS.**

AREPAS
500 g (1 lb 2 oz) masa flour
  (see Glossary)
2½ teaspoons fine sea salt
1½ teaspoons caster (superfine)
  sugar
40 ml (1¼ fl oz) olive oil
650 ml (22½ fl oz) warm water
2 litres (70 fl oz) cottonseed oil,
  for deep-frying

TO SERVE
500 g (1 lb 2 oz) queso fresco
  (fresh cow's milk cheese)
  (see notes)

BLACK BEAN SOFRITO

Either soak the black beans in cold water overnight or in cold water with a teaspoon of bicarbonate of soda (baking soda) for a minimum of 2 hours.

Once soaked, drain the beans then put them in a medium saucepan, cover with cold water, add a pinch of salt and bring to the boil. Turn down the heat, and simmer for about 1 hour, or until just cooked. Keep topping up the water as the beans cook so you have triple the amount of water to beans. Allow the beans to cool in the water they were boiled in.

Roughly chop the vegetables into 2.5 cm (1 inch) pieces — you can leave the chillies and garlic whole.

In a medium saucepan, heat the extra virgin olive oil over a high heat, then add the chopped vegetables, chillies and garlic. Reduce the heat to low–medium and cook for 30–40 minutes, stirring occasionally, until the vegetables are tender and just starting to break down.

Add the piquillo peppers and cook for 10 minutes more. Add the paprika and vinegar and cook out for a couple more minutes. Take the saucepan off the heat and leave the vegetables to sit in the pan for 10 minutes, so any slightly burnt bits from the base of the pan soften and become part of the paste.

Transfer the vegetable mix to a blender, puréeing in batches until smooth. Season to taste with salt then spoon into a clean saucepan. Cook over a low–medium heat until it's a really thick paste.

Strain the beans, add them to the paste with a little of their water and cook for a further 15–20 minutes. Ideally, you should now have a thick rich sauce, not a paste, so add a splash of water if it seems too thick.

Taste to check the seasoning then put aside. The sofrito should be room temperature before serving.

CORN PICO

Soak the corn cobs in their husks in cold water for 30 minutes to 1 hour then shake off the excess water. Preheat the barbecue to medium–high heat and barbecue the corn for 12–15 minutes, turning occasionally until the husks are burnt.

Put the corn in an airtight container with the lid on and set aside to steam for 30 minutes.

Remove and discard the husks and fibres. Remove the kernels with a sharp knife — be sure not to cut too close to the cob.

Combine the corn kernels with the rest of the ingredients, except the extra virgin olive oil, in a bowl. Mix everything together, season with salt and a good drizzle of extra virgin olive oil, and put aside until serving.

AREPAS

Mix the masa flour, salt, sugar and olive oil together in a bowl. Add the water and mix continuously with your hands to make a dough. Allow the dough to rest for 10 minutes.

Quarter the dough, then roll out each piece on non-stick baking paper to achieve the desired thickness — just under 1 cm (½ inch) is ideal as it will only expand a little, if at all.

Stamp out circles with a round cutter about 7 cm (2¾ inches) in diameter. You can also re-roll the offcuts.

Fill a large, deep heavy-based saucepan a third full (no more) with oil and heat to 180°C (350°F). Deep-fry the dough circles, adding one at a time to the oil and frying no more than three at a time. Fry for 3–4 minutes, turning once until golden. If they stick together, remove with a slotted spoon, carefully separate them then return to the oil for one more minute.

Drain on paper towel. Allow to sit for a few minutes before cutting open. You can keep any leftovers in the fridge and re-fry them.

TO SERVE

Cut each arepa in half horizontally, but not all the way through. Slice the queso fresco into thin rectangular strips and fry thesc in a small frying pan over a medium heat for 30 seconds on each side.

Put some sofrito, queso fresco and corn pico inside each arepa, and serve.

Buttermilk Pancakes

with Fried Bacalao, 62-Degree Eggs & Smoked Maple Butter

SERVES 8

Every time we go to the States we always have fried chicken and waffles for breakfast. After we renovated Bodega, we were thinking we needed to shake up the menu a bit with a sweet/savoury item you could happily eat for breakfast, lunch or dinner. You could even eat this for dessert. It was a little bit of a piss-take on the flash 62-degree eggs everyone does. We thought, 'Let's just put one of those on a pancake with fried cod on it.' The secret to making a good, fluffy pancake is self-raising flour, lots of salt and melted butter. The recipe has a few different components to it, but a few of them — such as the smoked butter (which is also delicious with scrambled eggs) and chilli maple syrup — can be made ahead of time and then stored.

BACALAO MIX
500 g (1 lb 2 oz) bacalao (salt cod), strips or belly pieces if you can find them (see Glossary)
1 litre (35 fl oz) milk
6 garlic cloves
2 fresh bay leaves
200 g (7 oz) potato
75 ml (2¾ fl oz) extra virgin olive oil

SMOKED MAPLE BUTTER
250 g (9 oz) chilled unsalted butter
80 ml (2½ fl oz) pure maple syrup
1 teaspoon fine sea salt
charcoal and hickory chips for smoking (see pgs 138–139)

NOTE: THE PANCAKE BATTER, BACALAO MIX AND SMOKED MAPLE BUTTER CAN ALL BE MADE THE NIGHT BEFORE.

BUTTERMILK PANCAKES
175 g (6 oz) cracked whole eggs
300 ml (10½ fl oz) buttermilk
1 teaspoon fine sea salt
1½ tablespoons caster (superfine) sugar
300 g (10½ oz) self-raising flour
100 g (3½ oz) unsalted butter, melted
250 g (9 oz) cold, cubed, unsalted butter (for clarifying)

62-DEGREE EGGS
8 eggs + 2 extra test eggs at room temperature

CHILLI MAPLE SYRUP
3 red bird's eye chillies
500 ml (17 fl oz) pure maple syrup

TO SERVE
cottonseed oil, for deep-frying
40 g (1½ oz) clarified butter (see method)
50 g (1¾ oz) smoked maple butter, softened (see method)
2 spring onions (scallions), greens thinly sliced, for garnish

BACALAO MIX

Cover the fish with water, soak in the refrigerator overnight, then rinse.

Submerge the fish in milk in a medium saucepan, add the garlic and bay leaves and bring to simmer over a medium heat. Simmer for 5 minutes then drain, keeping 55 ml (1¾ fl oz) of warm milk for later (discard the garlic and bay leaves).

Meanwhile, peel and cube the potato. Place in a small saucepan and cover with cold water. Bring to a simmer over a medium heat and simmer until tender.

Remove any skin and bones from the fish and place the flesh in a food processor. Pulse until fine then drizzle in the extra virgin olive oil and reserved warm milk, and pulse again until combined and emulsified.

Pass the warm potato through a ricer or push through a sieve then combine with the fish in a bowl and refrigerate until needed.

BUTTERMILK PANCAKES

In a large bowl, whisk the eggs and buttermilk with the salt and sugar.

Sift the flour into the bowl and whisk gently until just incorporated.

Drizzle in the melted butter, fold it through, then refrigerate until needed. Transfer to a large piping (icing) bag when ready to cook. (If you don't have a piping bag, you can just spoon the batter into the frying pan.)

CLARIFIED BUTTER

Cook the 250 g (9 oz) of cold, cubed unsalted butter in a small saucepan over a low–medium heat until the milk solids sink to the bottom of the pan and reach the point where they start sticking to the bottom.

Remove from the heat, pass the butter through a fine sieve then refrigerate until needed.

SMOKED MAPLE BUTTER

Slice the butter horizontally into three pieces. Place in a small tray lined with baking paper and cold smoke for 20–25 minutes (see pages 138–139).

Take out the butter; it should be chilled, but still quite pliable. Place in a small food processor with the maple syrup and salt and whip until combined. Store in an airtight container in the fridge until ready to use.

62-DEGREE EGGS

Set a circulating water bath to 62°C (144°F). Alternatively, you could heat a large saucepan of water to the same temperature and use a digital thermometer (and a simmer pad if you have one) to maintain the temperature the whole time. Gently add the eggs (whole) and cook for 1½ hours.

Remove one egg with a slotted spoon and carefully crack it into a small bowl — the white should be translucent and soft (scoop away any gelatinous white) and the yolk should be runny. If the white is not yet cooked enough, cook the others for an extra 5–10 minutes. Hold them at 60°C (140°F) until ready to serve.

CHILLI MAPLE SYRUP

Halve the chillies lengthways and put them in a small saucepan with the maple syrup.

Bring to the boil over a medium–high heat then turn down the heat and simmer for 2 minutes. Allow to stand until cool then transfer or pour into a container and reserve until needed. This will keep for up to 3 months in the fridge.

TO SERVE

Have the cooked eggs on hand, ready to serve. Preheat the oven to 160°C (315°F/Gas 2–3) if needed (to reheat the pancakes).

To fry the bacalao, fill a deep heavy-based saucepan a third full (no more) with the oil and heat it to 170–180°C (325–350°F).

Using a dessertspoon, scoop the bacalao mix into an egg shape and gently lower into the saucepan.

Fry in small batches for 3–5 minutes, or until they are a deep golden colour. Drain on paper towel.

In a large non-stick frying pan over a low–medium heat, put a tablespoon of oil and a quarter of the clarified butter. Once the butter begins to foam, pipe or spoon the pancake mix into the pan to give two pancakes about 10 cm (4 inches) in diameter (they will expand slightly). Once bubbles come through the batter (about 1–1½ minutes), flip the pancake and cook for a further minute then transfer to a baking tray lined with non-stick baking paper — arrange them flat, not stacked.

Wipe out the pan and repeat until you have eight pancakes. When ready to serve, flash the pancakes in the oven if needed.

Place on plates then rub each pancake with a teaspoon of smoked maple butter. Leave a little extra knob of butter to rest on top of each pancake.

One at a time, crack the 62-degree eggs into a small bowl. Then, using a slotted kitchen spoon, place an egg just off-centre on each pancake.

Place the bacalao beside each egg and drizzle over a tablespoon (or more if you like) of the chilli maple syrup. Finish with the sliced spring onion.

Barbecued Sweetbreads

with Buckwheat Noodles, Minced Prawns & Egg Sauce

SERVES 8

GINGER PICKLE

a large knob of ginger, roughly
    chopped
1 red bird's eye chilli, roughly
    chopped
1 long red chilli, roughly
    chopped
1 long green chilli, roughly
    chopped
250 ml (9 fl oz) rice wine
    vinegar
50 g (1¾ oz) fine sea salt
50 g (1¾ oz) caster (superfine)
    sugar

MINCED PRAWNS

500 g (1 lb 2 oz) raw tiger
    prawns, peeled and deveined
    (heads and shells reserved
    for the egg sauce)

EGG SAUCE

6 eggs, at room temperature
reserved prawn heads and
    shells from the minced
    prawns
250 g (9 oz) unsalted
    butter, chopped
soy sauce
caster (superfine) sugar
fine sea salt (optional)

BUCKWHEAT NOODLES
(SEE NOTE)

2 eggs
3 egg yolks
10 ml (¼ fl oz) olive oil
135 g (4¾ oz) buckwheat flour
135 g (4¾ oz) plain
    (all-purpose) flour, plus
    extra for dusting
pinch of fine sea salt

VEAL SWEETBREADS

400 g (14 oz) veal sweetbreads
vegetable oil
fine sea salt
juice of ½ a lemon

TO SERVE

extra virgin olive oil
15 g (½ oz) finely chopped
    chives
chilli oil (see pg 272)

NOTE: YOU CAN SUBSTITUTE
THESE NOODLES WITH 400 G
(14 OZ) OF FRESH EGG NOODLES
OR EVEN FRESH PASTA.

GINGER PICKLE

Place all of the ingredients in a small, deep saucepan over a high heat. Boil for 5 minutes, then cool and strain. Set aside until needed.

MINCED PRAWNS

Finely mince the prawn meat with a sharp knife. Place in a sieve and submerge in a saucepan of very salty boiling water for 5 seconds, or until it is just turning opaque. Use chopsticks to move it around.

Drain, then cool on a tray in the fridge.

EGG SAUCE

Set a circulating water bath to 62°C (144°F). Alternatively, you could heat a large saucepan of water to the same temperature and use a digital thermometer (and a simmer pad if you have one) to maintain the temperature the whole time. Gently add the eggs (whole) and cook for 1½ hours. If you aren't ready to use them straight away, hold them at 60°C (140°F) until you're ready.

Preheat the oven to 200°C (400°F/Gas 6). Place the heads and shells of the prawns in a flameproof roasting tray and roast them for 10 minutes, or until they are fragrant and red.

Place the tray over a medium heat and add the butter. Move everything around with a wooden spoon as the butter melts, and cook for a few minutes.

Pass the prawn shells and butter through a fine sieve into a bowl, crushing the shells with the wooden spoon to extract as much butter as possible.

Crack open the cooked eggs and place the yolks in a bowl (discard the whites). Whisk slowly, gradually adding the flavoured butter.

Season with a few drops of soy and a pinch of sugar, then taste and add some salt, if needed. Cover with plastic wrap then set aside in a warm place.

BUCKWHEAT NOODLES

Combine the wet ingredients in a jug and place the dry ingredients in a food processor. Turn the processor on and slowly add all of the wet ingredients. Process until just combined.

Lightly dust a clean surface with flour then knead your dough until it's smooth and springy.

Halve the dough and, working with one piece at a time, flatten it with your fingertips until it's thin enough to fit through the widest setting of your pasta machine.

Roll the dough through the pasta machine then lay it on the work surface, dust lightly with flour and fold each outside edge into the middle. Fold one side over on top, turn the dough 90 degrees and roll it through the pasta machine's widest setting again. Repeat this folding and rolling until the dough is

smooth then continue to roll the dough through the pasta machine, reducing the settings as you go and dusting with flour as necessary until it's about 1–2 mm (1/16 inch) thick. (You may need to cut the dough in half at some point depending on how much work space you have and how easy you find the dough to handle.)

Fit a spaghetti attachment to your pasta maker then feed the dough through, catching it on the other side as it emerges and dusting with more flour to prevent the noodles from sticking. Set aside.

In a large saucepan filled with salted, boiling water, blanch the noodles in two batches for 30 seconds to a minute until tender, then strain and submerge in icy cold water until cold. Strain and toss with a small amount of vegetable oil to prevent the noodles from sticking together. Set aside at room temperature.

VEAL SWEETBREADS

Clean the sweetbreads (trim the gristly bits but leave the fat) then drizzle them with vegetable oil and season.

Barbecue them slowly over low heat (see the cooking over fire guide on page 213) for 40 minutes to 1 hour, and drop the grill right at the end to help give them some more colour. Squeeze over some lemon juice.

TO SERVE

Cut the barbecued sweetbreads in slices just smaller than 1 cm (½ inch) and place them evenly in a row on the plates so they're slightly overlapping.

Season the noodles with salt and pepper in a bowl and twirl them onto a fork using your hand as a base to hold them in place; they should end up in a twisted length not more than 15 cm (6 inches) long. Lay the noodles over the sweetbreads.

In a bowl, mix the minced prawns with a splash of extra virgin olive oil, the chives and some ginger pickle, to taste. Spoon this over the noodles, then zig zag over some of the egg sauce and add a drizzle of chilli oil over the top to finish.

Devilled Eggs
with Ham & Dill Pickles

SERVES 8 (2 HALVES PER PERSON)

We were just messing around in the kitchen, making a mayo base using some 65-degree egg yolks and we were like, 'Let's make some devilled eggs.' You can do it at home in a pot with a thermometer as long as the water doesn't go above 65 degrees. We cook off a whole lot of hard-boiled eggs, then we sift some of the hard-boiled yolk through the slow-cooked yolk. It's really full-on but it's got this amazing texture — almost stretchy. That's the secret. Pipe it through a star nozzle and it'll hold beautifully. If you wanted to get really fancy you could even torch the mix and almost caramelise your yolk. You can't do too much more to them, though: a devilled egg should be simple.

HARD-BOILED EGGS

8 eggs

DEVILLED EGG MAYO

4 eggs, at room temperature

50 ml (1½ fl oz) Sriracha sauce

1 teaspoon smoked paprika

2 teaspoons curry powder

2 tablespoons hot English mustard

2½ tablespoons tomato sauce
(ketchup)

2½ tablespoons sherry vinegar

1 tablespoon fine sea salt

500 ml (17 fl oz) canola or other
vegetable oil

TO SERVE

4 dill pickles (pg 275), sliced
lengthways

24 thin slices of ham (see pgs
120–123)

100 g (3½ oz) devilled egg mayo
(see above)

> **NOTE: YOU'LL HAVE SOME DEVILLED EGG MAYO LEFT OVER BECAUSE IT'S HARD TO MAKE LESS, BUT THE LEFTOVER IS GOOD FOR MAKING DEVILLED EGG SANDWICHES.**

HARD-BOILED EGGS

Boil the eggs for 10 minutes in a large saucepan of boiling water then put them in a bowl of ice water to prevent them cooking further.

Peel the eggs and halve them crossways. Scoop out the yolks, being careful not to break the whites. Keep the yolks from four of the eggs for the devilled egg mayo.

DEVILLED EGG MAYO

Set a circulating water bath to 65°C (149°F). Alternatively, you could heat a large saucepan of water to the same temperature and use a digital thermometer (and a simmer pad if you have one) to help maintain the temperature the whole time.

Gently add the four uncooked eggs (whole) and cook for 1½ hours. Once cooked, carefully crack open the eggs and place the yolks in a bowl (discard the whites).

Put the Sriracha, paprika, curry powder, hot English mustard, tomato sauce, sherry vinegar and salt into a food processor with the egg yolks. (You aren't using the yolks from the hard-boiled eggs yet, that's further down!)

Turn the processor on at a low speed and slowly start adding the oil in a constant stream until it's all incorporated. It should look pink in colour and hold together.

Pass the four reserved egg yolks from the hard-boiled eggs through a fine sieve or potato ricer, then add these to the mix and pulse until smooth and combined.

Scoop the mix into a piping bag with a star nozzle.

TO SERVE

Place the 16 yolkless egg halves in the middle of a serving plate and arrange the dill pickles and ham around them.

Pipe the devilled egg mayo into the cavity of each egg white.

Barbecued Octopus

with Sausage Terrine, Hash Brown & Aioli

SERVES 8

SAUSAGE TERRINE
750 g (1 lb 10 oz) skinless pork
 shoulder, diced
750 g (1 lb 10 oz) skinless pork
 jowl, diced
6 g ($^1/_5$ oz) sodium nitrate
 (see Glossary)
12 g ($^2/_5$ oz) fine sea salt
12 g ($^2/_5$ oz) light brown sugar
3 g ($^1/_{10}$ oz) freshly ground
 white pepper
3 g ($^1/_{10}$ oz) coriander seeds,
 toasted and ground
75 ml (2¾ fl oz) water
canola oil spray

OCTOPUS
4 medium octopus
 (about 165 g/5¾ oz each)

HASH BROWNS
2 kg (4 lb 8 oz) desiree potatoes
2 teaspoons fine sea salt

TO SERVE
extra virgin olive oil
cottonseed oil, for deep-frying
aioli (see the tip on pg 274)
sweet smoked paprika
1 teaspoon finely diced
 preserved lemon (see pg 279)
1 spring onion (scallion), green
 ends only, thinly sliced
river salt flakes

SAUSAGE TERRINE

Pass the pork shoulder and jowl through a 1 cm (½ inch) mincing blade, alternating between the two cuts as you go to evenly mix them. The mincer will slightly emulsify the meat for you.

Pass the mince through again using an 8 mm (³/₈ inch) mincing blade.

In a separate bowl, mix the sodium nitrate, salt, sugar, pepper, coriander seeds and water until combined.

Pour this mixture over the mince then put on disposable gloves and use your fingers to mix and emulsify everything until well combined and almost pasty.

Spray a square 20 cm (8 inch) baking tin that's 4 cm (1½ inches) deep with canola oil. Line with plastic wrap then press and mould the sausage mix into the tin firmly and evenly. Slap your open hand firmly onto the terrine to remove any air pockets or bubbles.

Wrap the tin with plastic wrap ten times each way, then place in a cryovac bag and stab four holes into the terrine, piercing the plastic wrap through the cryovac bag. Place in another cryovac bag and vacuum on the longest setting — the high amount of vacuuming will press the terrine for you.

Make sure the terrine is sealed properly, then place it into a temperature controlled water bath and cook at 65°C (149°F) for 2 hours. Remove from the water and place in an ice bath to stop the cooking process. Allow to cool to room temperature then refrigerate overnight.

Carefully turn the terrine out of the tin. Cut it in half then slice eight 1 cm (½ inch) thick rectangles. Save the rest (see note).

OCTOPUS

Clean each octopus by getting rid of the head and keeping the tentacles. Gently wash the tentacles.

Bring a large saucepan of salted water to the boil and reduce to a simmer.

Dunk the tentacles from one octopus into the simmering water for 3 seconds, then lift out and repeat three times. Do this with each octopus. This will tighten and firm the skin. Reduce the heat to very low.

Add the tentacles and leave to sit in the hot water for 40 minutes, or until tender. This may require longer depending on their size.

Remove and portion the tentacles into separate pieces.

HASH BROWNS

Peel and steam the potatoes for 20 minutes, then set aside until just cool enough to handle.

Coarsely grate the potatoes (wear thick washing-up gloves for this) into a large bowl and add the salt.

Using your hands, work the mixture to release the starches; this will help bind it together. Press into a square 20 cm (8 inch) baking tin that's 4 cm (1½ inches) deep. Wrap tightly in plastic wrap then steam in a combination oven set to full steam (or use a large stovetop steamer) for 30 minutes.

Remove from the oven, unwrap the plastic and cover with more plastic wrap. Then, use an identically sized tray to press down onto the potatoes and refrigerate with a heavy weight on top. Leave for at least 2 hours.

After the potato has been pressed, carefully turn it out onto a chopping board and cut it in half. Slice one of the halves into eight 2.5 cm (1 inch) thick rectangles. Save the rest (see note).

NOTE: YOU'LL HAVE LEFTOVER SAUSAGE TERRINE AND HASH BROWNS, BUT THEY FREEZE REALLY WELL. DEFROST OVERNIGHT IN THE FRIDGE, AND THE NEXT MORNING YOU CAN FRY UP YOUR OWN VERSION OF A SAUSAGE MCMUFFIN WITH SOME SWEET MUSTARD SAUCE.

TO SERVE

Lightly oil the terrine slices with extra virgin olive oil. Skewer and lightly oil your octopus tentacles.

Preheat a coal barbecue or grill pan to medium–hot and lightly char the octopus as you warm the sausage terrine, barbecuing until golden brown on both sides.

Meanwhile, fill a medium heavy-based saucepan a third full (no more) with the cottonseed oil and heat it to 180°C (350°F). Fry the hash browns in batches for 3–4 minutes, or until golden all over.

Remove with a slotted spoon, drain on paper towel, then cut each hash brown into four pieces and season with salt.

Place a slice of sausage terrine on a plate and arrange your four hash brown pieces on top. Arrange some octopus tentacles leaning onto the hash brown.

Drizzle a few teaspoons of aioli over each portion of octopus and let it drip down onto the hash brown. Sprinkle over a small amount of smoked paprika, preserved lemon and green spring onion. Season lightly with salt then serve.

Mango & Fried Bread

with Lemon Sorbet & Salted Caramel

SERVES 8

LEMON SORBET

430 ml (15¼ fl oz) water

160 g (5¾ oz) dextrose
(see Glossary)

105 g (3½ oz) caster
(superfine) sugar

3 g (¹/₁₀ oz) microplaned lemon
peel

6 g (¹/₅ oz) ice-cream stabiliser
(see Glossary)

300 ml (10½ fl oz) freshly
squeezed lemon juice

SALTED CARAMEL

125 g (4½ oz) caster (superfine)
sugar

115 g (4 oz) liquid glucose
(see Glossary)

165 g (5¾ oz) cream (45% fat)

35 g (1¼ oz) unsalted butter,
chopped

canola oil spray

¼ teaspoon fine sea salt

110 g (3¾ oz) tapioca
maltodextrin (see Glossary)

TO SERVE

80 g (2¾ oz) clarified butter,
chopped (see pg 28)

8 × 4 cm (1½ inch) cubes of
white bread (or milk buns
(see pg 245), crusts removed

MANGO

2 ripe mangoes

1 tablespoon caster (superfine)
sugar

50 ml (1½ fl oz) white rum

CONDENSED MILK CREAM

250 ml (9 fl oz) cream (35% fat)

1 × 395 g (14 oz) tin of
condensed milk

2 teaspoons xanthan gum
(see Glossary)

LEMON SORBET

Bring everything (except the lemon juice) to 85°C (185°F) in a small saucepan over a medium heat, stirring to combine.

Chill overnight to let the flavours infuse.

The next day, strain and chill the lemon juice.

Strain the sugar mixture through a fine sieve then add the chilled lemon juice and blitz with a hand-held stick blender.

Churn the mixture in an ice-cream machine then freeze at -18°C (-0.4°F) until needed.

MANGO

Peel the mangoes and remove their cheeks and the sides (keep the stone). Cube the flesh and place it in a container.

Trim as much flesh as you can off the stone then blend that flesh with the sugar and rum, using a hand-held stick blender. Pour that over the diced mango, mix together then refrigerate.

SALTED CARAMEL (SEE NOTE)

Place the sugar, glucose, cream and butter in a small saucepan over a medium heat and stir to dissolve the sugar. Cook until it reaches 110°C (225°F).

Meanwhile, line a baking tray with baking paper and spray lightly with canola oil. Pour the hot caramel mixture onto the lined tray and leave to cool to room temperature. Refrigerate to chill then roughly chop into small pieces (it's a bit stretchy).

Add the chopped pieces to a food processor with the salt and tapioca maltodextrin, then pulse until they're all incorporated. Store in an airtight container at room temperature. This makes more than you need, but it's great sprinkled on ice cream.

CONDENSED MILK CREAM

Heat 50 ml (1½ fl oz) of the cream in a small saucepan over a medium heat until hot.

Place the condensed milk, xanthan gum and hot cream in a blender and mix until thick. Transfer to a bowl and refrigerate until it has set and is firm.

Place the firm mixture in a blender with the remaining cream and blend until glossy and smooth. Add a little more cream if necessary, to make it pipeable. Transfer to a piping (icing) bag and refrigerate until needed.

TO SERVE

Heat the clarified butter in a large non-stick frying pan over a low heat. Add the bread and fry on all sides until golden.

Place a cube of bread in the middle of each plate, spoon the diced mango over and around the bread. Pipe a few dollops of the condensed milk cream all around then spoon one or two scoops of lemon sorbet onto the plate and sprinkle with lots of the salted caramel. Repeat with the remaining ingredients.

NOTE: READ THE NOTE ABOUT TAPIOCA MALTODEXTRIN IN THE GLOSSARY BEFORE YOU MAKE THIS!

Banana Split

You can be guaranteed a flan in any bistro in Argentina so you never even need to look at the menu. Over there, it comes with whipped cream and dulce de leche. Our banana split is a bit of a take on that. The actual flan is the cream and then the dulce de leche element is the dulce de leche ice cream. The peanuts are the 'split'. This is a pretty complicated recipe, but plenty of the components, such as the flan and the dulce de leche ice cream, can be eaten as separate desserts. Even easier, come into Bodega and we'll make it for you. We took it off the menu for two weeks once because we were sick of making it, and there was anarchy. People were furious. Somebody even started a petition (we think it was Sarah).

CARAMEL
90 g (3¼ oz) caster (superfine) sugar
35 ml (1 fl oz) cold water
15 ml (½ fl oz) rice wine vinegar

FLAN
10 eggs, separated (keep 7 of the yolks for the ice cream)
150 ml (5 fl oz) milk
900 ml (31 fl oz) cream (35% fat)

BANANA MARSHMALLOW
260 g (9¼ oz) banana flesh (about 5 ripe unpeeled bananas)
16 g (½ oz) leaf gelatine (see Glossary)
250 g (9 oz) caster (superfine) sugar
85 ml (2¾ fl oz) cold water

SPICED BISCUIT
200 ml (7 fl oz) milk
165 g (5¾ oz) soft brown sugar
165 g (5¾ oz) honey
1¼ teaspoons baking powder
30 ml (1 fl oz) dark rum
30 ml (1 fl oz) Pernod or other aniseed liqueur
1 teaspoon ground coriander
1 teaspoon ground cinnamon
1 teaspoon ground nutmeg
1 teaspoon ground cloves
335 g (11¾ oz) plain (all-purpose) flour, sifted

DULCE DE LECHE ICE CREAM
50 g (1¾ oz) caster (superfine) sugar
splash of water
500 ml (17 fl oz) milk
250 ml (9 fl oz) cream (35% fat)
450 g (1 lb) dulce de leche
7 egg yolks (reserved from the flan)

REQUIRED AFTER BISCUIT IS MADE
75 g (2¾ oz) caster (superfine) sugar
80 ml (2½ fl oz) water

CARAMEL SAUCE
250 g (9 oz) caster (superfine) sugar
50 ml (1½ fl oz) cold water
½ a vanilla bean, split and seeds scraped
100 ml (3½ fl oz) rice wine vinegar

BANANA PURÉE
4 really ripe bananas, unpeeled
20 g (¾ oz) unsalted butter
1 tablespoon freshly squeezed lemon juice
3–4 tablespoons caster (superfine) sugar
150 ml (5 fl oz) cream (35% fat)

SALTED PEANUTS
150 g (5½ oz) unsalted peanuts
1 teaspoon fine sea salt
1 teaspoon extra virgin olive oil

CARAMEL AND FLAN

Put the sugar and water for the caramel in a very small heavy-based saucepan over a low heat, bring to the boil and cook until it starts to caramelise.

Once you have a light caramel colour, remove from the heat and add the vinegar to prevent any further cooking (be careful as it can spit).

Quickly pour into an 18 × 24 cm (7 × 9½ inch) ovenproof rectangle mould or tin about 6 cm (2½ inches) deep. Tilt from side to side to evenly cover the bottom. Cool to room temperature.

Preheat the oven to 140°C (275°F/Gas 1). Place the egg whites in a bowl with the milk and cream and whisk until just combined.

Pour this mixture evenly on top of the caramel and cover with foil. Place the mould or tin in a roasting tin and pour in enough hot water to come halfway up the sides of the mould. Bake for 1–1¼ hours, or until just firm. Uncover and leave to cool down at room temperature.

Once cool, remove the mould or tin from the roasting tin and transfer to the fridge to chill completely. Ideally, you'd leave it overnight as it can taste a little 'eggy' when eaten the same day.

BANANA MARSHMALLOW

Steam the bananas in their skins for 10–15 minutes. The skin should split in the middle and the flesh should be hot and soft all the way through.

While the bananas are steaming, place the gelatine leaves in cold water and let them soak for 5 minutes.

Mix the sugar and water together in a small heavy-based saucepan over a high heat, stirring to dissolve the sugar and bring to the boil. Boil until it reaches 125°C (257°F) to create a syrup.

While the sugar and water mixture boils, weigh the banana flesh in a bowl and blend with a hand-held stick blender until smooth.

Transfer the banana to an electric mixer bowl and, using the whisk attachment, whisk at the highest speed.

Turn the heat off once the sugar syrup has come up to temperature. Scoop the gelatine leaves out of the bowl and squeeze out any excess water before adding the leaves to the sugar syrup. Briefly stir through until dissolved and then carefully pour the syrup down the side of the mixing bowl (not directly onto the whisk) into the whisking bananas until it is all incorporated.

Whisk on high speed for 20–25 minutes, or until it is light and fluffy — meringue consistency.

Line a 21 × 26 cm (8¼ x 10½ inch) baking tray about 3 cm (1¼ inches) deep with baking paper and then pour in the marshmallow mixture. Spread it out evenly and then place non-stick baking paper over the top. Leave to cool to room temperature then refrigerate for 3–4 hours, or overnight if possible.

SPICED BISCUIT

Preheat the oven to 160°C (315°F/Gas 2–3).

Place all the ingredients for the biscuit, except the flour, in an electric mixer bowl and, using the paddle attachment, mix on a medium speed for 2 minutes to dissolve the sugar.

Turn the mixer off and add the flour. Turn the mixer back on but set it on a slow speed to combine, but not thoroughly mix, the flour in.

Line a 14 cm (5½ inch) square tin with non-stick baking paper and pour in the mixture, tilting the tin from side to side to spread it around evenly.

Bake for 1¼ hours until golden brown and fairly hard to the touch (it will crack slightly but that's OK).

Let it cool down then cut into three 4 × 11 cm (1½ x 4¼ inch) rectangles and trim until flat on top. Wrap individually in plastic wrap and freeze overnight.

Preheat the oven to 170°C (325°F/Gas 3). Unwrap the rectangles and slice them thinly (1–2 mm/ 1/16 inch thick) using a cold, sharp thin-bladed knife or meat slicer. You only need eight biscuits, but this recipe makes heaps.

Mix together the sugar and water. Lay the thin rectangles of biscuit on baking trays and brush them lightly with the mixture. Bake them for

5–10 minutes to crisp them up, they will turn slightly darker.

Let them cool down, then store in an airtight container between sheets of baking paper to ensure they don't stick together. Save the leftover biscuits to eat with ice cream another time.

DULCE DE LECHE ICE CREAM

In a small, deep heavy-based saucepan, combine the sugar with enough water to just dampen the sugar. Place the saucepan over a medium–high heat and put a small bowl of water and a pastry brush nearby so you can periodically paint a water line just above the sugar line — this is to prevent sugar splashing on the side of the saucepan and forming crystals in your mix. Boil until the sugar is all dissolved and you have caramel, swirling the pan gently to get an even colour.

Meanwhile, in a separate small saucepan, heat the milk and cream over a low–medium heat until just warm then add that to the caramel syrup, and whisk to combine.

Whisk in the dulce de leche and bring the mixure to the boil.

In a large bowl, whisk the egg yolks then slowly pour the caramel mix into the eggs, continuing to whisk until combined.

Strain into a container and cool overnight in the fridge.

Follow the manufacturer's instructions to churn your ice cream. Freeze at -18°C (-0.4°F) until needed.

CARAMEL SAUCE

Place the sugar, water and vanilla bean and seeds in a small, deep heavy-based saucepan over a low heat and stir to dissolve the sugar. Increase the heat slightly to bring to the boil and cook until it starts to caramelise. Continue to boil the mixture until you achieve a dark brown colour. Once the mixture is dark and starts to bubble rapidly, remove it from the heat.

Add the vinegar slowly (be careful as it can spit); you can always use a lid to shield yourself between pours.

Let the sauce cool down completely, remove the vanilla bean then pour into a squeeze bottle for use later.

BANANA PURÉE

Steam the bananas in their skins for 10–15 minutes. The skin should split in the middle and the flesh should be hot and soft all the way through.

Place the flesh in a blender with the butter, lemon juice and 3 tablespoons of the sugar, and blend for around 10 seconds.

Add the cream and blend for another 10 seconds. Taste and add the remaining tablespoon of sugar if you like.

Place the purée in a container and let it cool to room temperature before placing in the fridge.

SALTED PEANUTS

Preheat the oven to 150°C (300°F/Gas 2).

Spread the peanuts on a baking tray and roast for 25–35 minutes, or until they're a nice golden colour. Check them frequently and give them a quick toss every time.

Pour the nuts into a large bowl, add the salt and extra virgin olive oil, then toss until coated. Put the nuts back onto the tray and allow them to cool. Once cool, store in an airtight container.

PLATING UP

Smear a spoonful of the banana purée in the middle of each plate and run the back of the spoon through it to spread it out slightly.

Slice the flan into eight 4 × 11 cm (1½ x 4¼ inch) rectangles and do the same with the banana marshmallow. Place a slice of flan on each plate and top with a slice of marshmallow. Caramelise it with a kitchen blowtorch then top with a rectangle of spiced biscuit. Drizzle over some of your caramel sauce then sprinkle a few peanuts on top and beside the flan.

Place a scoop of dulce de leche ice cream next to the banana split, or on top of the peanuts (try to place it so it doesn't slide off). Serve immediately.

Chocolate Pudding

with Coffee Fernet Sabayon, Mandarin Ice Cream & Olive Crumbs

SERVES 8

DEHYDRATED OLIVES

150 g (5½ oz) drained and
    pitted kalamata olives

MANDARIN ICE CREAM

125 ml (4 fl oz) milk

100 ml (3½ fl oz) cream
    (35% fat)

80 g (2¾ oz) skim milk powder

150 g (5½ oz) dextrose
    (see Glossary)

30 g (1 oz) caster (superfine)
    sugar

8 g (¼ oz) ice-cream stabiliser
    (see Glossary)

2 g (²/₂₅ oz) microplaned
    mandarin peel

450 ml (16 fl oz) freshly
    squeezed mandarin juice

30 ml (1 fl oz) freshly squeezed
    lemon juice

OLIVE CRUMBS

35 g (1¼ oz) dehydrated olives
    (see left)

35 g (1¼ oz) smoked pecans
    (see pg 139)

75 g (2¾ oz) soft brown sugar

½ teaspoon ground star anise

½ teaspoon ground cardamom

35 g (1¼ oz) dark chocolate
    (64% cocoa solids), roughly
    chopped

COFFEE FERNET SABAYON

4 g (⁴/₂₅ oz) leaf gelatine
    (see Glossary)

200 g (7 oz) caster (superfine)
    sugar

300 g (10½ oz) egg yolks

300 ml (10½ fl oz) espresso

70 ml (2¼ fl oz) Fernet Branca

8 g (¼ oz) xanthan gum
    (see Glossary)

CHOCOLATE PUDDINGS

150 g (5½ oz) dark chocolate
    (64% cocoa solids), roughly
    chopped

150 g (5½ oz) unsalted
    butter, chopped, plus extra
    (softened) for greasing

3 eggs

120 g (4¼ oz) caster (superfine)
    sugar, plus extra for dusting

120 g (4¼ oz) plain (all-
    purpose) flour

5 g (⅛ oz) baking powder

15 g (½ oz) unsweetened
    cocoa powder

DEHYDRATED OLIVES

Pat the olives dry with paper towel before evenly layering them in a dehydrator set at 50°C (122°F) for 24 hours. If you don't have a dehydrator, spread them in an even layer on a baking tray and dry in the oven at 140°C (275°F/Gas 1) for 4 hours, or until dried. If you're making semi-dried olives, they'll only need 2 hours.

MANDARIN ICE CREAM

Bring everything (except the citrus juices) to 85°C (185°F) in a saucepan over a medium heat, stirring to combine.

Chill overnight to let the flavours infuse.

The next day, strain and chill the citrus juices.

Strain the cream mixture through a fine sieve then add the chilled citrus juices and blitz with a hand-held stick blender.

Churn your ice cream in a machine following the manufacturer's instructions. Freeze at -18°C (-0.4°F) until needed.

OLIVE CRUMBS

Pulse the olives in a food processor to get them as small as possible without turning them into a paste. Transfer to a bowl, then do the same with the pecans. Add them to the olives. (Don't combine any of this in the food processor.)

Add the brown sugar, star anise and cardamom to the bowl and rub with your fingers until everything comes together.

Pulse the chocolate in the food processor then add to the bowl. Mix lightly and store in an airtight container in the fridge.

COFFEE FERNET SABAYON

Soak the gelatine leaves in cold water until softened. Whisk the sugar and egg yolks together by hand. Add the espresso and the Fernet Branca then transfer to a saucepan and cook over a medium heat, whisking constantly, until thick and boiling. It will look split but will be fine later.

Squeeze any excess water from the gelatine then add to the mixture with the xanthan gum. Pour everything into a container then blend with a hand-held stick blender until it resembles thick custard. Pour it into a cream gun and charge it twice. Keep upside down and do NOT refrigerate.

CHOCOLATE PUDDINGS

Place the chopped chocolate and butter in a heatproof bowl over a saucepan of simmering water. Make sure the base of the bowl is not in contact with the water. Stir occasionally until completely melted.

Place the eggs and sugar in the bowl of an electric mixer fitted with a whisk attachment. Whisk until light and doubled in volume. Transfer to a bowl, add the chocolate mixture and fold through straight away. Sift in the flour, baking powder and cocoa then fold through.

Grease eight 7 cm (2¾ inch) diameter ramekins (approx. 135 ml/4½ fl oz capacity) with softened butter. Dust each ramekin with sugar and tip out any excess.

Spoon the pudding mixture into the moulds then wrap each one in plastic wrap and steam in a steamer basket over a saucepan of boiling water for 15 minutes, or until the pudding is just set on the outside, but soft on the inside.

TO SERVE

Carefully turn the puddings out onto serving plates, then pump some coffee Fernet sabyon from the cream gun next to each pudding.

Give the sabayon a quick go with a blowtorch, sprinkle the olive crumbs over and around the puddings. Scoop the ice cream onto the olive crumbs next to the puddings and serve right away.

Praline & Chocolate Pudding

with Milk Ice Cream & Frozen Apple

SERVES 8

MILK ICE CREAM
500 ml (17 fl oz) cream
(35% fat)
67 g (2⅓ oz) trimoline (invert
sugar syrup) (see Glossary)
150 g (5½ oz) liquid glucose
(see Glossary)
1½ teaspoons fine sea salt
500 ml (17 fl oz) milk

LEMON PURÉE (SEE NOTES)
3 lemons
1 kg (2 lb 4 oz) caster
(superfine) sugar
1 litre (35 fl oz) cold water

CHOCOLATE PUDDING
230 g (8½ oz) dark chocolate
(64% cocoa solids), chopped
230 g (8½ oz) unsalted butter,
chopped
7 eggs
300 g (10½ oz) caster
(superfine) sugar
100 g (3½ oz) plain (all-
purpose) flour

HAZELNUT FILLING
125 g (4½ oz) hazelnut paste
(see notes)
100 ml (3½ fl oz) cream
(35% fat)
100 ml (3½ fl oz) milk
105 g (3½ oz) caster
(superfine) sugar
3 g (¹/₁₀ oz) fine sea salt
2½ g (²/₂₅ oz) leaf gelatine
(see Glossary)
1 egg yolk
1 egg
20 g (¾ oz) unsalted butter

FOR GARNISH
1 green apple
juice of ½ a lemon

HAZELNUT PRALINE
100 g (3½ oz) caster (superfine)
sugar
20 g (¾ oz) unsalted butter
65 g (2⅓ oz) hazelnuts, roasted
and peeled
a pinch of fine sea salt

TO SERVE
135 g (4¾ oz) roasted and
peeled hazelnuts

NOTES: BUY A HAZELNUT PASTE
THAT HAS A MINIMUM AMOUNT
OR, BETTER YET, NO ADDED
SUGAR. ALTERNATIVELY YOU
CAN MAKE YOUR OWN BY
ROASTING 150 G (5½ OZ) OF
HAZELNUTS AT 200°C (400°F/
GAS 6) FOR 5–6 MINUTES. RUB
OFF THEIR SKINS IN A TEA
TOWEL, COOL SLIGHTLY THEN
BLITZ TO A PASTE IN A SMALL
FOOD PROCESSOR.

THE HAZELNUT FILLING AND
THE LEMON PURÉE MAKE
MORE THAN YOU NEED,
BUT THE LEFTOVERS ARE
GREAT ON TOAST.

MILK ICE CREAM

Bring everything (except the milk) to the boil in a medium heavy-based saucepan over a medium heat, stirring as it heats.

Pour the mixture into a bowl, add the milk then blitz with a hand-held stick blender and cool to room temperature. Chill overnight in the fridge.

The next day, blitz again and churn your ice cream in a machine following the manufacturer's instructions. Freeze at -18°C (-0.4°F) until needed.

LEMON PURÉE

Put the whole lemons into a medium saucepan and cover with cold water. Bring to the boil over a high heat, then change the water and repeat the process another five times.

Meanwhile, in another medium heavy-based saucepan, mix the sugar with the litre of cold water.

After the final change of water, use a slotted spoon to move the boiled lemons to the sugar mixture and bring that to the boil. Discard the lemon water.

Turn the heat down and simmer gently until the liquid has reduced by half and the lemons take on a candied appearance — their peel should be translucent and shiny and the liquid should be thick.

Remove from the heat. Once cool enough to touch, remove the lemons from the liquid then halve and deseed them.

Place the lemons and some of their cooking liquid in a blender and blend to obtain a runny consistency (it should just hold on to a spoon), adding more liquid as needed.

Once the purée cools down, it will thicken up. Store in a sterilised jar in the fridge for up to a month.

CHOCOLATE PUDDING

Place the chocolate and butter in a heatproof bowl over a saucepan of simmering water. Make sure the base of the bowl is not in contact with the water. Stir occasionally until completely melted.

Meanwhile, crack the eggs into a clean bowl.

Once the chocolate and butter have melted, remove the bowl from the heat.

Add the sugar to the eggs, whisk together, then gradually add the chocolate and butter mixture and whisk fairly rapidly.

Sift in the flour and fold it through the mixture. Cool slightly.

Transfer the mix to a piping (icing) bag and leave in the fridge for 2–3 hours.

HAZELNUT FILLING

Put the hazelnut paste, cream, milk, 60 g (2¼ oz) of the sugar and the salt in a saucepan over a high heat. Stir every minute or so until it all comes together and is hot.

Soak the gelatine leaves in a small bowl of cold water to soften.

In a separate bowl, whisk the egg yolk, whole egg and remaining sugar. Whisking continuously, gradually add the hot hazelnut sauce to the egg mixture until it is all incorporated. Pour this mixture back into the saucepan then cook over a high heat, whisking continuously, until the mixture starts to bubble and thicken.

Squeeze the excess water from the gelatine leaves and whisk the gelatine into the mixture along with the butter.

Once all the ingredients are combined, cool slightly then transfer to a piping bag and leave in the fridge to cool completely.

FOR GARNISH

Peel the apple, cut into quarters and deseed. Wrap in plastic wrap and place in the freezer. You can brush it with a little lemon juice before freezing to stop oxidation if you like.

HAZELNUT PRALINE

Heat the sugar with a splash of water in a small, deep heavy-based saucepan over a low heat. Cook to a caramel consistency and colour, gently shaking the pan occasionally for even colour. The sugar should be completely melted and not too dark in colour.

Remove from the heat, whisk in the butter then add the hazelnuts and salt.

Ensure it is mixed well then pour onto a lined baking tray and let it cool completely.

Once cooled, break into pieces and pulse to fine crumbs in a food processor. Store in an airtight container.

STEAMING THE PUDDING

Spray the insides of eight 7 cm (2¾ inch) tins, ramekins or pudding moulds (approx. 150 ml/ 5 fl oz capacity) with oil. Pipe a thick layer of the chocolate pudding mix into each tin to cover the bottom.

Pipe about a tablespoon worth of hazelnut filling into the centre of each chocolate base, then pipe more chocolate around and on top of that, encasing the hazelnut filling and making sure there is still a 5 mm (¼ inch) gap from the top.

Wrap all of the tins in plastic wrap and steam in a steamer basket over a saucepan of boiling water for 25–35 minutes, or until the puddings are cooked on the outside and some of the chocolate mixture is still soft on the inside.

TO SERVE

Smear some lemon purée on one side of each plate.

Put some of the roasted hazelnuts on top of the purée — this will act as an anchor for the ice cream.

Unwrap the steamed puddings and carefully loosen them around the edges with a small knife.

Flip them out onto the plates, next to the purée.

Sprinkle some hazelnut praline on the top of each pudding.

Scoop out an ice-cream ball and place on the roasted hazelnut and lemon purée.

Grate some frozen apple on top to finish.

David Chang's
RECIPE FOR A GOOD TIME

Recipe Haiku

cold beer and blue crabs
celebrate late summer sun
heavy on Old Bay

THE PERFECT *Picnic*

Outside of a picnic, there's no other situation, really, where you can have your car, your food and your friends all in one place. We love picnics. They're a chance to catch up, put on a great outfit and spend time with friends. And the best part of all is that everyone brings that one thing they do really well; you find yourself looking forward to having a slice of this person's cake, or a glass of that person's special punch. That dinner-party pressure of doing it all yourself is gone because you're all chipping in to create a party.

But a great picnic isn't even necessarily just about the food — it's a chance for everyone to show off their Sunday best: the vintage cars come out, the girls go the extra mile to make sure their hair is perfectly set and everyone competes for the title of best picnic basket.

We wanted to re-create the perfect picnic and share some of the stuff we like to do. But, as is so often the way with picnics, on the day the weather turned against us and it rained. This turned out to be a good thing because it reminded us how crucial it is to have a solid back-up plan.

This is where understanding friends with nice houses and big driveways come in. It's easy enough to relocate all of the picnic stuff to a decent-sized backyard, and then you've got somewhere to clean the dishes, retouch your hair and play records. Ultimately, it doesn't matter whether it's in a park or a house — it's the hanging out and having a good time that counts.

The Motors

Yep, the cars are pretty important. Everyone always does something extra special to their car to get it ready. It's as much about checking out what everyone else is driving as it is rolling up in your own ride. It's not that often you get to see that many old cars together in one place outside of a car show, and it's a treat for us to see each other's rides, too. Ideally, the weather will play along on the day. If not, the Buicks, the Caddies, the Chevys, the Holdens and the Valiants all stay in. They're old cars, with vacuum-pressure windscreen wipers, which take about an hour to get going, so they only come out if the sun's shining. It's pretty cool to pick people up along the way, too. It's a big procession.

The Outfits

Getting ready for the picnic is almost as exciting as the picnic itself. Everyone comes in their best picnic outfits and their most inappropriate picnic shoes, then everyone tries to outdo each other with their picnic baskets. It's all in good fun though, and we keep it friendly.

Some of our friends are really authentic about their baskets, and their picnic blankets match their clothes, which match their car. Sarah's the expert when it comes to picnic clothes: 'You'd probably wear capris to be practical — you can sit down without worrying about flashing anyone your knickers,' she says, 'but it's always spectacular to wear a big skirt and petticoats so you can spread out. And if you're going to eat a lot you want to be comfortable and have the space to hide all you've eaten. For summer, it's all about beautiful skirts, hats and sunglasses. The boys just wear jeans and cowboy boots. Of course, some of the girls wear jeans or shorts, and some of the guys go all-out and wear high-waisted pants, Hawaiian shirts . . . Elvis and Ben don't really give a damn and will turn up in whatever. No thongs! (Or at least that's what they tell their mates.)'

The Food

It's important to bring food you can hold in one hand and walk around with. We like to make our own bread, brisket and ham (see the Handmade chapter, pages 96–139). That said, not everyone has time to smoke their own ham or bake their own bread, so it's also totally fine to buy the bits and pieces and just assemble it yourself. The Pineapple Princess (on pages 76–77) is the perfect example of assembling on location. She's a classic '50s dish, and will always turn heads when you show up with her. Prepare all the skewers for her at home, put them in containers, then once you get to the picnic, you (ahem) poke the princess. You can reload her as many times as necessary, then chop her up and eat her when you're done.

In true picnic style, everyone brings their own food and shares. There are always a lot of pies and cakes. With that in mind, we always like to have a barbecue going (it's easy if you choose a park with a barbecue already there) for chorizo, and our house-smoked bacon (page 124). You can even take a piece of brisket (pages 130–133) and grill that too.

One of our favourite sandwiches is our take on Elvis Presley's sandwich of choice, Fool's Gold. His version was a whole white Italian loaf, brushed in a stick of butter, baked till it's all golden and crisp, then filled with a jar of grape jelly, a jar of peanut butter and a tonne of fried bacon. Our version is significantly smaller, but you should definitely Google his sometime.

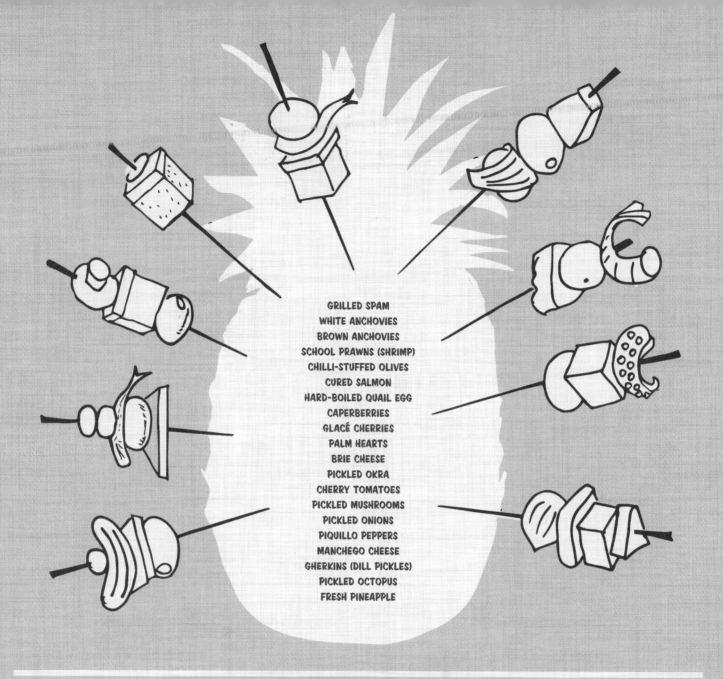

GRILLED SPAM
WHITE ANCHOVIES
BROWN ANCHOVIES
SCHOOL PRAWNS (SHRIMP)
CHILLI-STUFFED OLIVES
CURED SALMON
HARD-BOILED QUAIL EGG
CAPERBERRIES
GLACÉ CHERRIES
PALM HEARTS
BRIE CHEESE
PICKLED OKRA
CHERRY TOMATOES
PICKLED MUSHROOMS
PICKLED ONIONS
PIQUILLO PEPPERS
MANCHEGO CHEESE
GHERKINS (DILL PICKLES)
PICKLED OCTOPUS
FRESH PINEAPPLE

Pineapple Princess Tips

A pineapple princess is all about using what you've got on hand
in your fridge and cupboard, and making whatever combos you want.

Use good-quality skewers that aren't too long or too short. Plastic swords are a no go.

Choose a good solid pineapple that has a nice flat bottom.

Don't push your skewers too far into the pineapple otherwise
people won't be able to pull them out easily, and it'll fall over.

Have designated skewers for meat and vegetarian.

Make sure the ingredients for the skewers are all cut roughly the same size.

Don't overload your skewers or you'll stab the back of your
throat as you're trying to get at that last morsel!

Pineapple & Passionfruit Cheesecake

SERVES 8-10

ANZAC CRUMB BASE

150 g (5½ oz) plain (all-purpose) flour

125 g (4½ oz) rolled oats

70 g (2½ oz) caster (superfine) sugar

90 g (3¼ oz) desiccated coconut

1 teaspoon fine sea salt

150 g (5½ oz) unsalted butter, diced

200 ml (7 fl oz) pure maple syrup

3 g (1/10 oz) bicarbonate of soda
   (baking soda)

CHEESECAKE MIXTURE

500 g (1 lb 2 oz) cream cheese,
   chopped

200 g (7 oz) caster (superfine) sugar

2 eggs

200 ml (7 fl oz) cream (35% fat)

50 ml (1½ fl oz) passionfruit purée
   (see note)

50 ml (1½ fl oz) pineapple purée
   (see note)

ANZAC CRUMB BASE

Preheat the oven to 180°C (350°F/Gas 4).

Mix the flour, oats, sugar, coconut and salt together in a large bowl.

Melt the butter and maple syrup together in a small saucepan over a low heat and add the bicarbonate of soda.

Add the melted butter mixture to the dry ingredients, mix together well then use your hands to bring it all together.

Grease a 20 cm (8 inch) spring-form cake tin and line it with baking paper, then press the crumb into the base and bake for 15 minutes. Set aside to cool to room temperature.

CHEESECAKE

Turn the oven down to 130°C (250°F/Gas 1).

Beat the cream cheese and sugar in the bowl of an electric mixer, fitted with a paddle attachment, until smooth.

With the mixer running, add the eggs and cream and mix for a further 2 minutes.

Pour the mixture into the tin, evenly covering the biscuit base, then drizzle over the fruit purées and use a skewer to gently swirl them through the mixture.

Bake for 1 hour, or until just set.

Allow to cool to room temperature and then chill before eating.

NOTE: FRUIT PURÉES ARE AVAILABLE FROM SPECIALTY FOOD STORES, OFTEN IN TETRAPACKS.

Burger & Sandwich Suggestions

CHEESEBURGER
Beef patty
Cheese
Pickle
Mustard
Tomato sauce (ketchup)

BRISKET 'N' CHEESEBURGER
Brisket
Cheese
Pickle
Onion
Mustard
Tomato sauce (ketchup)

FOOL'S GOLD SANDWICH
Bacon (belly)
Crunchy peanut butter
Grape jam
Melted butter (for brushing
over the buns)

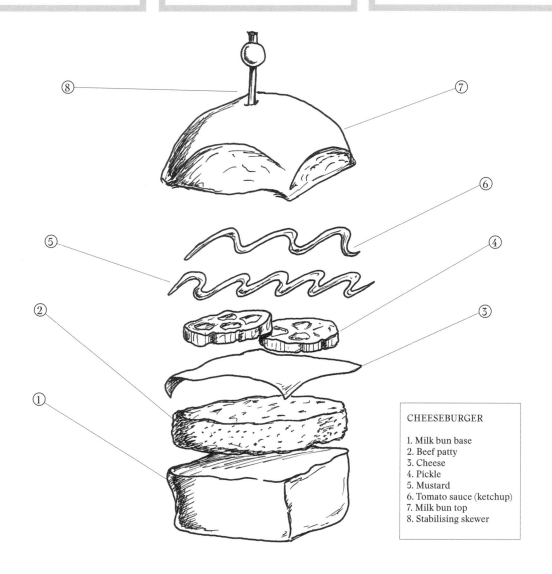

CHEESEBURGER

1. Milk bun base
2. Beef patty
3. Cheese
4. Pickle
5. Mustard
6. Tomato sauce (ketchup)
7. Milk bun top
8. Stabilising skewer

Sweet Potato Tarts

MAKES 24

The sweet potato filling for these tarts never tastes the same twice so follow the instructions below, have a taste before you fill the tarts and adjust the flavour, if needed; it's right when it tastes amazing. Eat any leftover filling as it is, as a side with roast dinner, or even smeared on toast, if you like.

CINNAMON PASTRY CASES
1 × cinnamon pastry (see pgs 176–177)
unsalted butter, for greasing
uncooked rice or baking beans,
　for blind baking

PIE FILLING
500 g (1 lb 2 oz) sweet potato, peeled
　and cut into chunks
200 ml (7 fl oz) pure maple syrup
200 g (7 oz) unsalted butter, chopped
200 ml (7 fl oz) water
60 ml (2 fl oz) cream (35% fat)
freshly grated nutmeg, to taste

JD MAPLE GLAZE
55 g (2 oz) soft brown sugar
250 ml (9 fl oz) pure maple syrup
a pinch of fine sea salt
60 ml (2 fl oz) Jack Daniel's whiskey

TO SERVE
crème fraîche

CINNAMON PASTRY CASES
Lightly grease 24 round tart tins about 5 cm (2 inches) in diameter and 1.5 cm (⅝ inch) deep.

Once you've prepared and chilled the pastry, remove it from the fridge and divide it into four. Roll out each portion of dough (one at a time) on a floured work surface until it's 2–3 mm (⅛ inch) thick. Use an 8.5 cm (3½ inch) diameter cutter to cut out rounds. Working carefully (the pastry is quite delicate), press the pastry rounds firmly into the base and side of your tart tins. Use a knife to trim away any excess pastry then arrange the tart tins on two trays and refrigerate for 30 minutes.

Preheat the oven to 160°C (315°F/Gas 2–3). Remove the tart cases from the refrigerator, line each one with a double layer of plastic wrap then fill with uncooked rice or baking beans and twist the plastic wrap to seal.

Blind bake for 15 minutes then remove the rice and plastic wrap and bake the tart cases for another 5–10 minutes, or until the pastry is golden. Leave to cool.

PIE FILLING
Put the diced sweet potato into a medium saucepan and just cover with the maple syrup, butter and water.

Gently simmer over a low–medium heat for 25–30 minutes, or until the sweet potato has broken down. Transfer to a food processor and blitz with the cream and a few gratings of nutmeg. Set aside and leave to cool.

JD MAPLE GLAZE
Put all of the ingredients in a small heavy-based saucepan, bring to the boil, simmer for a few minutes then set aside to cool.

TO SERVE
Fill each tart case with about 1½ tablespoons of sweet potato filling and spoon over some of the JD maple glaze. Top each tart with a teaspoon of crème fraîche and serve.

Jelly

FLAVOUR COMBOS

GLACÉ CHERRY JELLY
WITH CHOPPED GLACÉ CHERRIES

BLUEBERRIES IN BLUEBERRY JELLY

GIN AND TONIC JELLY

STEWED-STRAWBERRY JELLY ON TOP

POACHED RHUBARB
IN RHUBARB JELLY

ALMOND MILK JELLY

RASPBERRIES IN PEACH
AND CHAMPAGNE JELLY

GINGER, YOGHURT
AND CREAM JELLY

RASPBERRIES AND BLUEBERRIES
IN STEWED BERRY JELLY

PLUM JELLY WITH A SPLASH
OF COGNAC

TIPS FOR GOOD JELLY

We always use gold- or titanium-strength gelatine leaves to help the jelly set really well (see the Glossary for further explanation).

We use ingredients we have on hand (see the jelly combos here for ideas) and whatever seasonal fruit is available.

We find poached fruit works better than fresh fruit because it has a softer texture and you can use its cooking liquor to help flavour and set the jelly. The jelly stops the fruit from oxidising so it will last longer once set in the jelly. Just be aware that fresh fruit can sometimes make a jelly break down faster so if you go that route, it's best to serve it within a day of making it.

When layering your jelly, it's a good idea to put the moulds in a large container filled with really icy water. This helps the jelly to start setting while you're working. Make sure the first layer is pretty much fully set before adding the next. And be sure the next layer you pour is chilled, not warm, or else they will bleed into one another.

To set fruit in a jelly, pour 5 mm (¼ inch) of jelly onto an already set layer of jelly and allow to set just enough to be tacky; this will act like glue and help the fruit to stay in the desired place. Arrange your fruit then pour the balance of that layer of jelly around and over the fruit; this will stop the fruit from floating.

Once the jelly has set, be patient tipping it out of its mould. Lower the mould into a bath of hot water for a few seconds, or just until the jelly starts to separate from the side of the mould. Remove from the water bath, place a serving plate on top of the mould then flip it upside down and gently turn the jelly out onto the plate.

Boozy Banana Cake

SERVES 8-10

Elvis's mum started making this cake as a way of using up the leftover bananas from our banana old fashioneds (see page 261). We'd all come into the restaurant in the mornings and there'd be this boozy cake sitting there, covered in cream. Sometimes it's so boozy you have a bite and it literally takes your breath away and makes you screw your face up, but in a good way. The quantities for the bananas are pretty loose because we make the cake to taste. But generally, the batter should be quite wet before you add the flour, and the banana and booze flavours should really come across (unless you're making this for kids, in which case you can sub in ripe mashed bananas for the booze-soaked ones). We say eat it when you don't have to drive anywhere.

3 large bananas, sliced and soaked in 300 ml (10½ fl oz) of Jack Daniel's whiskey for 3 days then strained (strained weight approx. 350 g/ 12 oz)

150 g (5½ oz) unsalted butter, plus extra for greasing

250 g (9 oz) caster (superfine) sugar

5 eggs, separated

finely grated zest of 1 orange

finely grated zest of 1 lemon

300 g (10½ oz) plain (all-purpose) flour, plus extra for dusting

¼ teaspoon baking powder

¼ teaspoon bicarbonate of soda (baking soda)

TO SERVE (ALL OPTIONAL)

dulce de leche

whipped cream

crème fraîche

Preheat the oven to 150°C (300°F/Gas 2). Grease and lightly flour a 20 cm (8 inch) round bundt tin (or whatever tin you want to cook this in: loaf, spring-form etc.).

Put the paddle attachment on an electric mixer then cream the butter and sugar together in the mixer bowl until light and fluffy. Add the egg yolks to that mixture, one at a time, then all of the strained boozy bananas. Continue to beat for a few minutes, or until the batter is smooth, loose and creamy.

Whisk the egg whites in a clean bowl until soft peaks form. Add the orange and lemon zest to the batter. Sift the flour, baking powder and bicarbonate of soda together then fold that through the banana mix with a spoon. Fold through the egg whites until combined.

Pour the batter into the prepared cake tin and bake for 35–45 minutes, or until a skewer inserted in the centre comes out clean. Leave to cool a little then serve with your favourite cake condiments.

Elvis's mum cuts her cake in half horizontally, smears dulce de leche on it, then puts the top back on like a sandwich and finishes it with whipped cream. But Elvis reckons the sweet potato filling from the tarts on page 84 could also be amazing in there, and Ben likes the idea of using the JD maple glaze, also on page 84, on top. It's up to you.

The Drinks

Ben is always in charge of the bar. If he had things his way, every drink would have Passiona in it. You need to take plenty of Eskys on a picnic, and you need one just for ice. It's always a good idea to buy everything cold on the way to the picnic, too. If you stop at a service station and buy all your mixers already cold, it's going to be easier to keep them that way. And split up the jobs: one person brings the beer and another brings the ice, spirits and all the gadgets to mix some drinks. You could keep your spirits in the freezer, too, so everything's nice and cold — especially if you're necking it neat. The most important thing is to keep everything you make really simple. Punches are good because they're social, and everyone stands around the punchbowl and has a chat. Ben's signature move is the TCB Punch (the secret is Passiona, naturally). The Pineapple Princess (page 77) can also double as a sneaky drink if you like; hollow out the middle, fill it with rum or vodka and you've got an instant cocktail. She's a versatile dame.

TCB Punch

This is Ben's invention, which debuted at a house party back when we were all living in Redfern. TCB punch, short for Taking Care of Business, is just a combo of lots of different soft drinks but the most important components, of course, are Passiona (the mightiest of the passionfruit-flavoured soft drinks), tinned fruit and syrup. Our barmen spend forever making these syrups that you pour in your cocktails, but we figure those fruit tins just come with their own. It's pretty cool to freeze the fruit beforehand, so it breaks down and keeps the punch cold.

1 watermelon
2 × 750 ml (26 fl oz) bottles of vodka
1.25 litre (44 fl oz) bottle of Passiona
    (see note)
1.25 litre (44 fl oz) bottle of lemonade
1.25 litre (44 fl oz) bottle of ginger ale
2 litres (70 fl oz) mixed fruit juice
500 g (1 lb 2 oz) tinned mixed fruit in
    syrup
250 g (9 oz) strawberries
150 g (5½ oz) raspberries
ice, to serve

Cut open the watermelon in a design you like, making sure the opening is big enough for a ladle. Core out the melon, keeping the flesh and juices to add to the punch later.

Mix all the liquid ingredients in a large separate jug or container, then add the tinned fruit and all of its syrup.

Hull and slice the strawberries. Dice the watermelon flesh into pieces just slightly larger than the raspberries.

Add some fruit and plenty of ice to the watermelon shell, then pour in enough of the vodka mixture to fill it up. Top up as needed.

Get some glasses and suckitdown.

Wait for the party to start.

NOTE: PASSIONA IS A CARBONATED PASSIONFRUIT DRINK.

HANDMADE

We've never been big on molecular cooking. Don't get us wrong —
we love eating it, just not cooking it. Perhaps because our sausage-like
fingers can't hold tweezers.

We've always been fascinated by handmade products: sausages, cured
meats and fish, and the process of smoking and baking. It's what we love to
eat the most. We aren't too keen on reading for research, so most of our recipes
are created by trial and error. When we first started making our own chorizo
at Bodega, it was a disaster. Who knows how many batches we ruined? And
there's only so much bolognaise, larb and meatballs you can stomach. We
finally got it right and we reckon our chorizo is pretty tasty. From then, it was
on: what else could we make? Bacon, ham, blood sausage . . .

It was hard back then because we were limited by space; Bodega only has
a bar and kitchen combo. A few years later when we opened Porteño, we
wanted to put the emphasis on making as many products in-house as
we could. It was a point of difference because our products weren't going to
taste like anyone else's. We push ourselves to learn and it's fun. So now we
make a few types of bread each day as well as pâté, sausage, ham, salami,
bacon, smoked fish and cheeses.

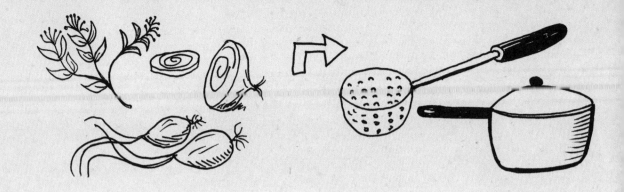

The recipes in this chapter are very basic. We like the brine method for most of our curing, for evenness. Flavour-wise, we've decided to leave it up to you because we are always changing how we spice things depending on the type of dishes we want to create with them. Plain is our favourite way to go because then it doesn't get too confusing.

Please feel free to play around with ratios and spices, or try honey, molasses or maple syrup in the brines instead of sugar (or leave out the sweet element completely if you like). Remember, you can always add more to a dish but it's harder to take it away. The most important thing is to taste the product and learn to make it exactly the way you want it. That's really what handmaking your own ingredients is all about.

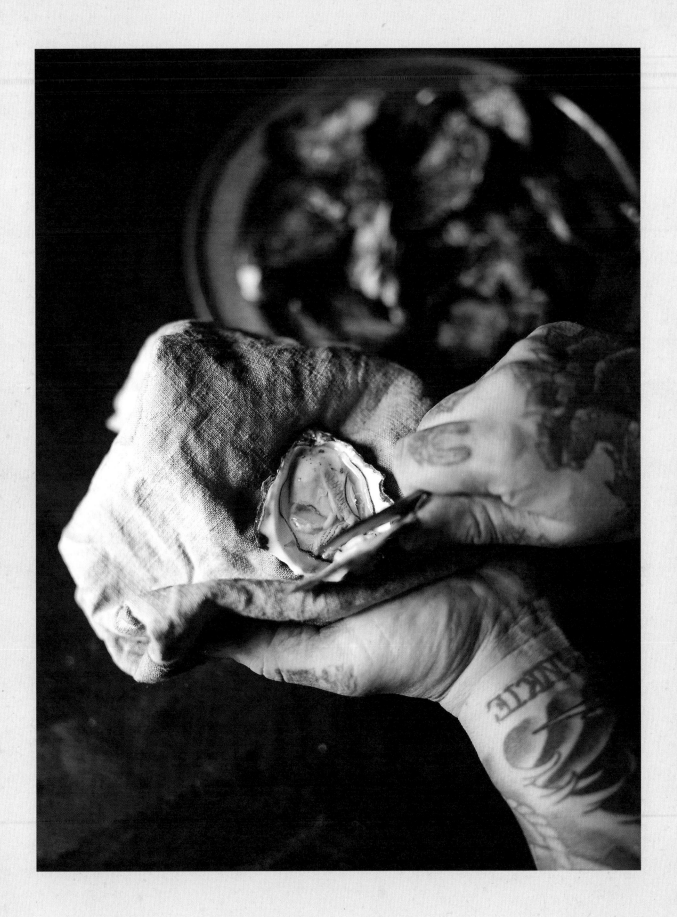

PAN DE CASA

Makes 12 rolls

THE STARTER

225 ml (7¾ fl oz) water
2 g (²/₂₅ oz) fresh yeast
225 g (8 oz) strong flour

BREAD DOUGH

320 ml (11 fl oz) lukewarm water
8 g (¼ oz) fresh yeast
the starter (from above)
550 g (1 lb 4 oz) strong flour,
    plus extra for dusting
20 g (¾ oz) fine sea salt
olive oil, for greasing

— 1 —
THE STARTER
Combine the water and yeast in a medium mixing bowl until there are no lumps. Add the flour and mix with a wooden spoon until evenly combined. The mix will be very wet and gluey. Cover with plastic wrap then poke a couple of holes in the top. Sit in a warm place (20–28°C/68–82°F) overnight.

THE "STARTER" MUST BE PREPARED THE NIGHT BEFORE YOU WANT TO MAKE THE DOUGH!

2
MAKING THE DOUGH

The next day, whisk the water and yeast together making sure that there are no lumps. Pour the starter you made yesterday into the bowl of an electric mixer fitted with a dough hook. Add the flour and salt. Begin mixing while slowly adding about half of the combined water and yeast. Mix for about 2 minutes before slowly adding the remaining combined water and yeast.

3

Continue mixing the dough for another 5–10 minutes, or until it is smooth and elastic. It should also be wet and sticky.

4

Generously oil a plastic container or loaf (bar) tin about 13 × 20 cm (5 × 8 inches) and 9 cm (3½ inches) deep. Place the dough in the container, cover with lightly greased plastic wrap and allow to prove for 2 hours. The dough should double in size.

5

TURNING THE DOUGH

To achieve a good rise when baking this bread, it is important to turn the dough as it proves. Turning the dough strengthens it and traps air inside so it becomes light and airy as it bakes. After the dough has proved for 2 hours, roughly spread 2 or 3 handfuls of flour evenly over a clean work surface.

6

Turn the dough out onto the floured surface, taking care to keep the rectangular shape. Carefully slide your hands under the dough and stretch it out to twice the length but try to keep the rectangular shape and not knock too much height out of the dough.

7

Dust the surface of the dough with flour and then brush off any excess flour with a large pastry brush. Fold the dough back onto itself in thirds, first in one direction (side to side), and then the other (top to bottom). Press the dough gently with your fingers as you do this.

8

Oil the container again then return the dough to the oiled container. Cover with the lightly greased plastic wrap and allow to prove for 1 hour. When the time is up, turn the dough again by repeating steps 5–7. Oil the container once more, put the dough back in and cover it with the greased plastic wrap. Allow to prove for a further 1½ hours.

↓

↓

9
SHAPING THE DOUGH

Make sure that the work surface is heavily floured and gently turn the proved dough out on to it. Carefully stretch the dough out to approximately 21 × 28 cm (8¼ x 11¼ inches). Dust with flour then use a pastry cutter to divide the dough evenly into twelve squares roughly 7 cm (2¾ inches).

10

Place the portions of dough on two baking trays lined with baking paper, floured sides up. Allow to prove, covered loosely (a clean garbage bag opened right out works well) in a warm environment approximately 25–35°C (77–95°F) for 1–1½ hours.

11
BAKING THE DOUGH

Preheat the (fan-forced) oven to 250°C (500°F/Gas 9) and place a small ovenproof saucepan of boiling water inside it.

Uncover the trays of proved dough and place them in the oven. After 3 minutes, drop the temperature to 220°C (425°F/Gas 7). Continue to bake for 15–18 minutes, or until the bread has a golden crust.

↓

↓

FETA CHEESE

Makes about 400 g (14 oz)

Making your own cheese is actually really simple, and once you see how easy it is, you'll want to do it again and again. We reckon Melbourne-based online store Cheeselinks (cheeselinks.com.au) is one of the best resources for anyone wanting to make cheese in Australia. You can order absolutely everything you need for this on their website, and it will show up on your doorstep in one little starter kit a few days later. It's great.

FETA

100 ml (3½ fl oz) full-fat UHT milk
  (see Glossary)
1 g (¹/₂₅ oz) type A culture
  (see Glossary)
2 litres (70 fl oz) full-cream non-
  homogenised goat', sheep' or cow's
  milk (we use Jersey milk)
0.3 g (¹/₁₀₀ oz) vegetarian rennet
  (see Glossary)
3 ml (¹/₁₀ fl oz) boiled then
  cooled water

BRINE

2 litres (70 fl oz) water
65 g (2⅓ oz) fine sea salt

MARINADE

1 litre (35 fl oz) light olive oil
4 fresh bay leaves
a few black peppercorns

1
MAKING THE FETA

Combine the UHT milk with the type A culture and allow the mixture to incubate at a constant environment of about 25°C (77°F) for 8 hours, until set like a soft yoghurt. (This could take between 8 and 16 hours if the temperature drops lower.) The culture can then be covered and stored in the fridge for up to 48 hours.

2

Place the full-cream milk in a large sterile, stainless steel saucepan and whisk in the culture. Place over a low heat and bring up to 32°C (90°F). It is essential to keep the milk at this temperature. To do this, you can keep the saucepan in a larger saucepan or tray that has a pool of water at 32°C. You can top that water bath up with more hot water, as needed, to regulate the temperature. Constantly check the temperature of the water and adjust the heat as needed.

3

Add the rennet to the cooled water then whisk that mixture into the milk for about 2 minutes, but no longer than 3 minutes.

4

Cover the saucepan with plastic wrap and maintain at 32°C (90°F) for 1–1½ hours while the mixture sets. Remember to keep checking the temperature of the water bath and milk.

5

Remove the saucepan from the water bath and, using a long, sharp sterile knife, cut the curds into 2 cm (¾ inch) squares while still in the pan by cutting the curd vertically in one direction and then horizontally. Cover the pan with plastic wrap and allow to stand for another 45 minutes.

6

Use a large sterile kitchen spoon to gently stir the curds and ladle out as much of the whey as you can. Let the curds sit for 1 hour, then stir again and gently pour away as much of the whey as you can. Carefully pour the curds and remaining whey into a basket or sieve lined with a large piece of muslin (cheesecloth). Fold over the muslin as you press down on top of the curd.

7

Place the wrapped curds in a basket suspended over a small bucket or deep bowl. Put a plate and a heavy weight on top of the curds then press in the fridge overnight so the whey can drain off.

8
BRINING

The following day, place the water for the brine into a saucepan with the salt, bring to the boil, then allow to cool completely. Transfer to a sterile bowl. Take the cheese out of the fridge and, leaving it in the muslin, place it in the cooled brine. Refrigerate for 24–48 hours depending on how salty you like your cheeses.

9
MARINATING

In a small saucepan, heat 200 ml (7 fl oz) of the light olive oil with the bay leaves and peppercorns. Once hot, remove from the heat, cool then add to the remaining 800 ml (28 fl oz) of light olive oil. Take the cheese out of the brine, pour the brine away and allow the cheese to sit for 5 minutes so any excess brine can drain off.

10

Remove the cheese from the cloth, cut or break it into the desired portion sizes and place in the flavoured oil to marinate. Store in the fridge at least overnight before using. If you are patient, let it marinate for 1 week. It can last up to 3 weeks.

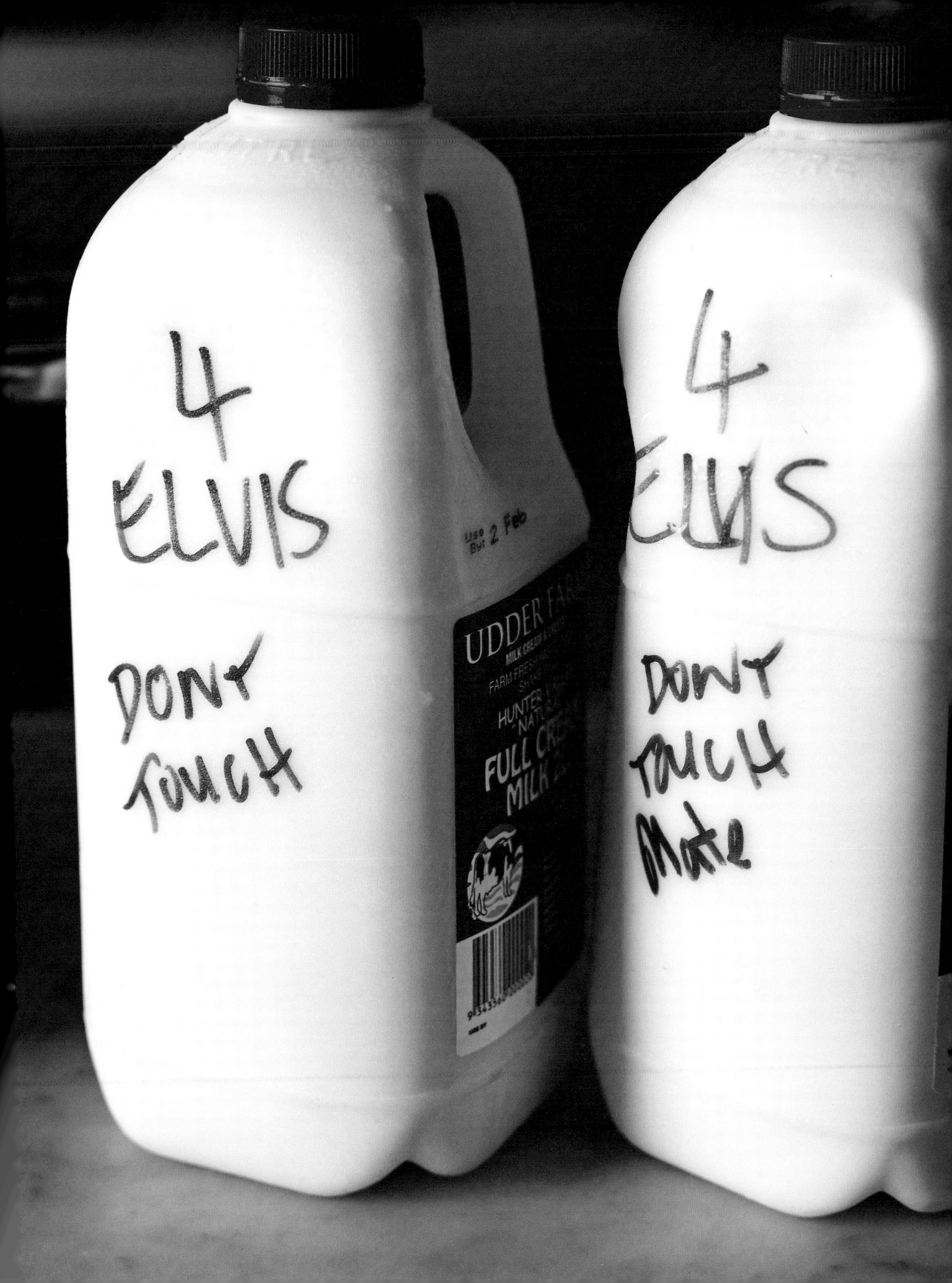
4
ELVIS
DONT
TOUCH
Use By 2 Feb
4
ELVIS
DONT
TOUCH
Mate

PORTEÑO CHORIZO

Makes 25 chorizo sausages

This recipe could be halved, but since the sausages keep really well in the freezer we think it's worth making a big batch and just storing any extra links in the freezer until you need them. It's really important to the end result that you use fresh, dry meat for this — not vacuum-sealed meat. Another tip is that we prefer using meat from a female pig because we find meat from a male pig often smells quite strong. This is known as boar taint.

CHORIZO FILLING

2.5 kg (5 lb 8 oz) pork shoulder, skin off and bone removed
2.5 kg (5 lb 8 oz) pork jowl, skin removed
   (ask your butcher to do this for you;
   if trimming yourself, you'll need 3.5 kg/
   7 lb 14 oz of pork jowl)
10 g (¼ oz) sodium nitrate (see Glossary)
45 g (1¾ oz) fine sea salt
40 g (1½ oz) smoked paprika
40 g (1½ oz) finely minced garlic
1 large nutmeg, finely grated
200 ml (7 fl oz) dry white wine
about 5 metres (just over 16 ft) of salted,
   natural, thick sausage skins

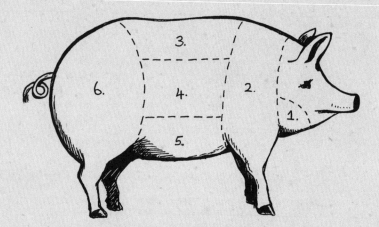

1. Jowl
2. Shoulder
3. Loin
4. Ribs
5. Belly
6. Ham

1
MAKING THE FILLING

It's important that the meat is well chilled and that you work in a cool environment when making these. Remove any skin remaining on the pork shoulder and use your hand to feel for any rough sinew or bone left on the underside of the meat. Remove that with a sharp boning knife. Slice the shoulder into long strips that will fit into the feeding spout of your mincer. Repeat this process with the pork jowl, but keep the two cuts of pork separate.

2

Set your mincer up with the largest mincing attachment. Feed the pork shoulder and jowl through the mincer, alternating from one to the other each time you feed a piece of meat through. This will evenly combine the leaner meat of the shoulder with the gelatinous fatty jowl.

3

Once all the meat has been minced, run it through the mincer again. This will incorporate the two cuts further and also start to emulsify the meat. The mince should be a chunky, but well-mixed, consistency. You don't want it too fine as this will stop your chorizo from developing the texture that you're trying to achieve in your finished product.

↓

↓

4

In a bowl, mix your mince with the sodium nitrate, salt, paprika, garlic, nutmeg and wine. Use your hands to really mix all of the dry ingredients evenly through the mince and emulsify the mixture.

5
FILLING THE SAUSAGE

Rinse any excess salt off the skins, and untangle them from their bundle. Get yourself two buckets of lukewarm water and fill each skin with a small amount of water. Run the skin between your fore-finger and thumb then feed it into the second bucket of water. This will remove any air pockets. Leave the open end of the skin hanging over the edge of the bucket so you can easily find it later.

6

Fill your sausage maker with the mince mix and follow the manufacturer's instructions. While filling your sausages, feed the mince into your casings slowly, ensuring there are no air pockets. If you have any, these can be removed after you've filled the sausage by piercing the skin with a sharp pin. Your chorizo should be firm, but not too firm or it will break open when you twist them later.

↓

↓

↓

↓

As your casing fills with mince, coil the filled sausage into a spiral with one hand on a clean, wet work surface. This makes it easier to control the firmness of the sausage as it is being fed out of the sausage maker.

=== 8 ===

LINKING & HANGING

Pinch and twist one way and then pinch and twist the opposite way so you're creating 15 cm (6 inch) sausages. These sausages then need to be linked. The linking of the sausages is really important because it helps them stay together. Saying that, it's really hard to explain in words how it's done, so our advice is to watch a couple of clips online about how to link sausages. There are heaps of good ones on YouTube.

=== 9 ===

Hang the linked sausages in the refrigerator for two days, or place them on trays lined with clean, disposable kitchen cloths (Chux). Make sure they aren't touching and are loosely covered so they dry out a little. Essentially, this chorizo is used fresh — not aged and dried — so it needs to be cooked before you eat it. Use within 4–5 days, or freeze until needed and defrost overnight in the fridge before using.

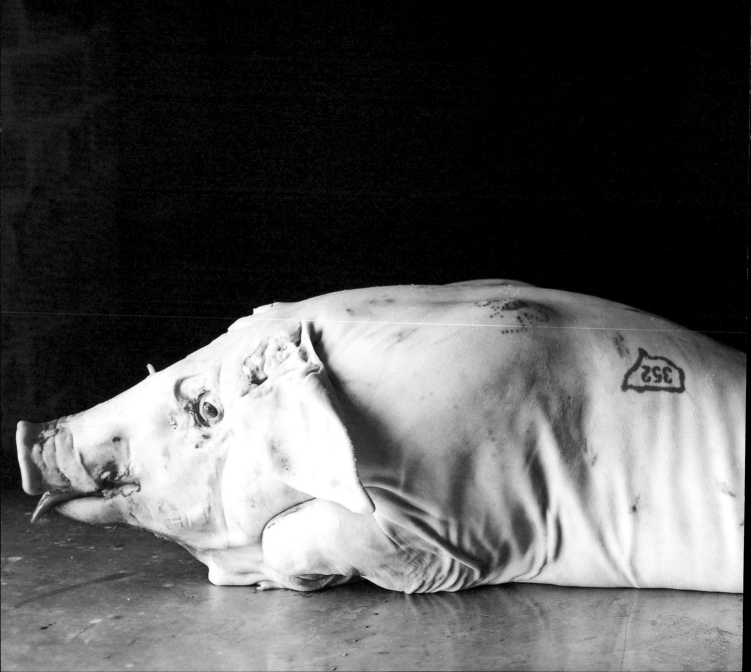

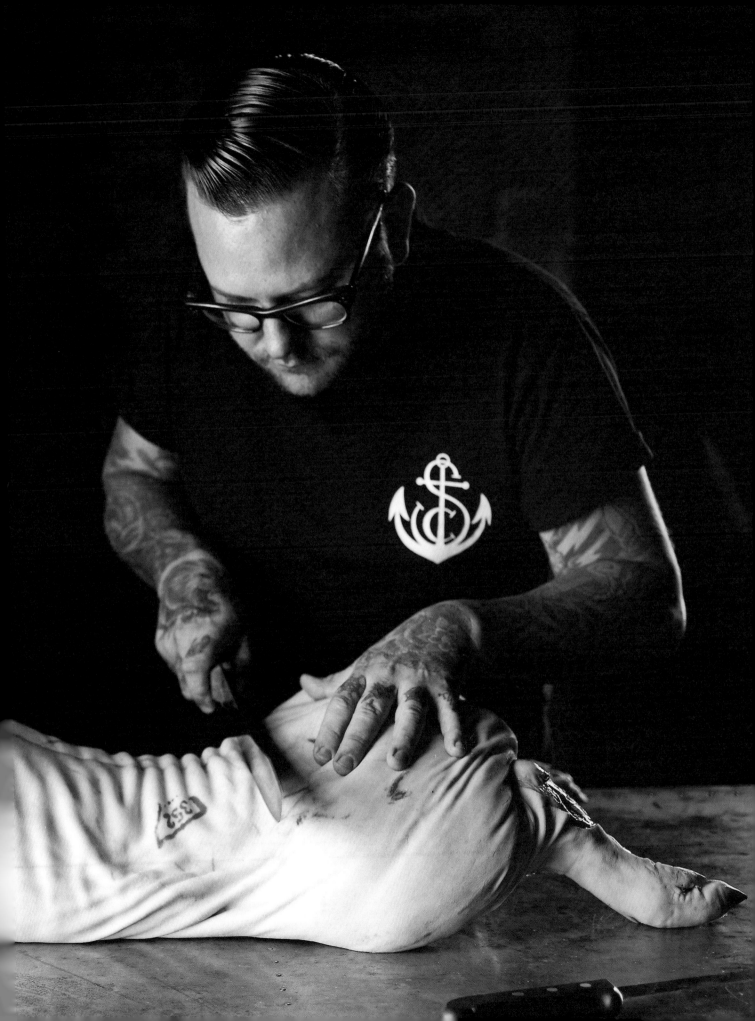

SMOKED HAM

Makes a 3 kg (6 lb 12 oz) ham

1 × 3 kg (6 lb 12 oz) leg of ham
   (we like using weaner pigs)
charcoal and wood chips, for
   cold smoking (see pgs 138–139)

BRINE

4 litres (140 fl oz) water
300 g (10½ oz) fine sea salt
325 g (11½ oz) brown sugar
40 g (1½ oz) sodium nitrate
   (see Glossary)

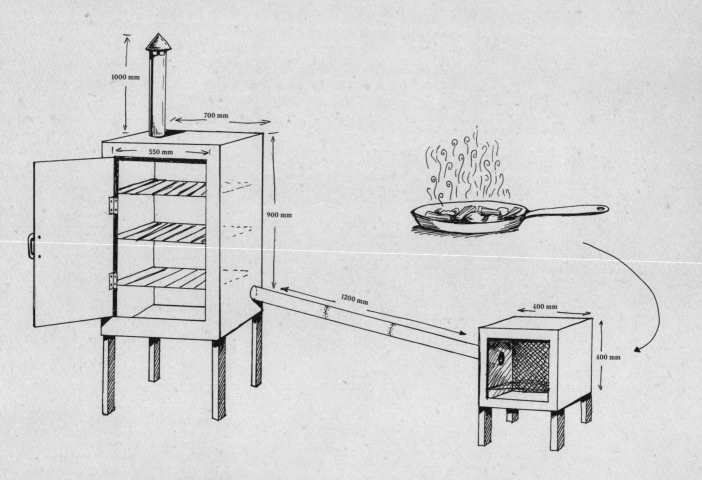

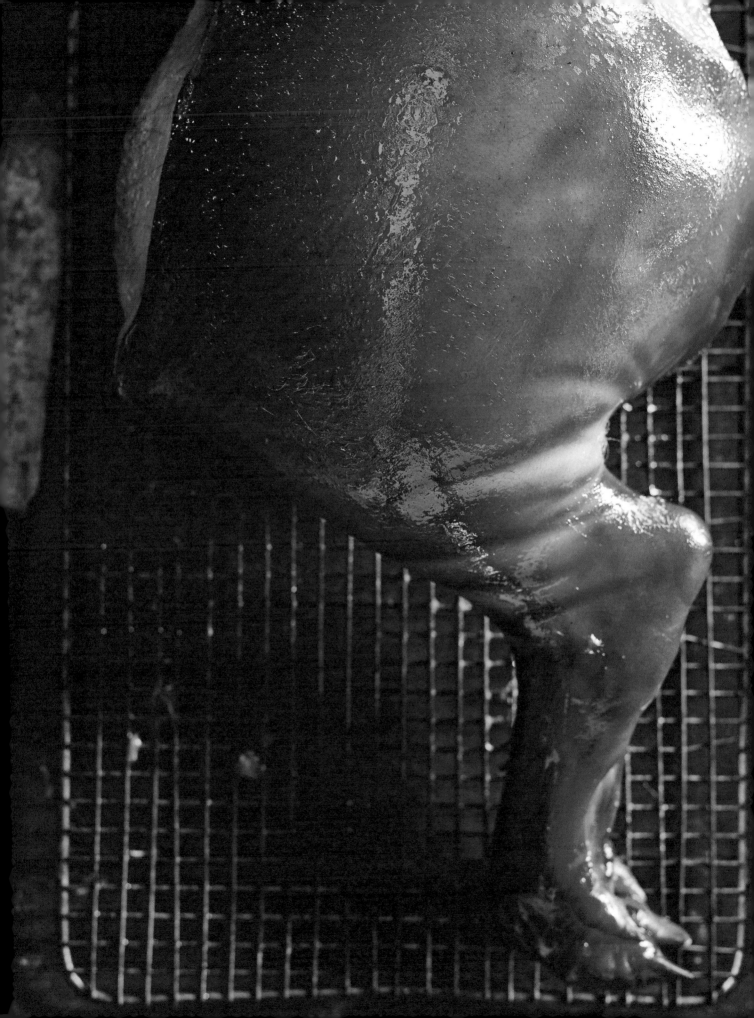

1
BRINING

Trim and discard any excess fat and veins from the leg. Whisk all the brine ingredients together in a large non-reactive tub or bucket until the salt and sugar have dissolved. Put the leg in the brine and place a weight on top to keep it fully submerged. Cover and refrigerate for 3 weeks.

2
DRYING & SMOKING

When ready, remove the leg from the brine, pat dry, then place on a wire rack over a tray and leave uncovered in the fridge overnight. Cold smoke the ham (see page 138) for 3 hours, replacing the wood and charcoal every hour.

↓

3
COOKING

Preheat the oven to 70°C (158°F/Gas ¼) and place the leg in the oven until the internal temperature reaches 68°C (154°F) (this will take about 4 hours). Remove from the oven, leave to cool to room temperature then refrigerate overnight. This will keep for up to 1 month, refrigerated. Slice thinly and serve.

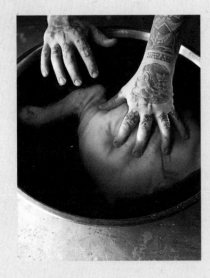

↓

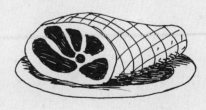

BACON

Makes 3 kg (6 lb 12 oz) bacon

1 piece of 3 kg (6 lb 12 oz) pork belly
   (preferably from a female pig),
   bone in
a tablespoon of your favourite spices
   (optional)
charcoal and wood chips, for cold
   smoking (see pgs 138–139)

BRINE

4 litres (140 fl oz) water
375 g (13 oz) fine sea salt
250 g (9 oz) brown sugar
30 g (1 oz) sodium nitrate
   (see Glossary)

1
BRINING

Whisk all the brine ingredients together until combined and add any spices, if using. Place the pork in a non-reactive container, then pour the brine over the pork until it's fully submerged. Place a weight on top if need be then cover with a lid and store in the fridge for 10 days.

2
DRYING & SMOKING

Remove the pork from the brine and pat dry. Place on a wire rack over a tray and leave uncovered in the fridge to dry out overnight. The next day, cold smoke the pork (see page 138) for 3–4 hours, adding extra wood and charcoal at least three or four times during the process.

3
COOKING

Preheat the oven to 90°C (195°F/ Gas ½) and place the belly in the oven to cook for about 3 hours, or until the internal temperature reaches 68°C (154°F). Allow to cool in the refrigerator overnight before slicing and eating. Wrap any unused bacon in plastic wrap and store in the fridge for 2–3 weeks, or in the freezer for up to 2–3 months. If frozen, be sure to defrost thoroughly in the fridge overnight before cooking.

PORK LIVER PÂTÉ

Makes about 600 g (1 lb 5 oz)

ONION AND SHERRY BASE

50 ml (1½ fl oz) olive oil
10 g (¼ oz) chilled unsalted butter
1 brown onion, finely chopped
fine sea salt and freshly ground black
  pepper
60 ml (2 fl oz) Amontillado sherry

PÂTÉ MIXTURE

190 g (6¾ oz) chilled unsalted butter,
  cubed
40 ml (1¼ fl oz) olive oil
500 g (1 lb 2 oz) pork livers, trimmed
  and cut into 4 cm (1½ inch) cubes
½ a nutmeg, for grating

— 1 —
MAKING THE BASE

Put the olive oil and butter in a
small saucepan or frying pan over
a low–medium heat. Add the onion
and cook, stirring occasionally, for
25 minutes, or until translucent.
Season with some salt and pepper
then add the sherry and cook until
it has almost all reduced. Pull the
pan off the heat and allow to cool.

2
MAKING THE PÂTÉ

In a large frying pan, gently heat 40 g (1½ oz) of the butter and the olive oil over a low heat. Add the liver and cook for about 2–3 minutes, turning once, until they are lightly coloured and pink in the middle. Be sure to season with salt and pepper as they cook.

3

Once the livers are cooked, tip them (and their buttery cooking juices) into a bowl and allow to rest. Chop the livers in a food processor in two batches (or more if you have a small food processor) until smooth. While mixing, gradually add the remaining cubes of cold butter and all the juices from the bowl — alternating between them as you go.

4

Once complete, spoon the mixture into a large bowl. Use a fine grater or microplane to grate over the nutmeg and season to taste. Add the cooled onion base and stir well.

5

Check for seasoning. If the mix is too thick, add a little splash of water and fold it through. The pâté should just fall off a spoon (it will firm up once refrigerated). Pour into a container, cover with plastic wrap and refrigerate to set. This will keep for up to 1 week. Serve with rolls, the water crackers on page 239, or whatever you like to eat pâté with.

SMOKED WAGYU BRISKET

Makes 2.5 kg (5 lb 8 oz)

1 × 2.5 kg (5 lb 8 oz) piece of wagyu brisket
charcoal and wood chips, for
   cold smoking (see pgs 138–139)
blended oil (95% canola + 5% extra virgin),
   for brushing over

BRINE

4 litres (140 fl oz) water
350 g (12 oz) fine sea salt
90 g (3¼ oz) brown sugar
225 g (8 oz) caster (superfine) sugar
40 g (1½ oz) sodium nitrate
   (see Glossary)
60 g (2¼ oz) honey

=== 1 ===
BRINING

Whisk all the brine ingredients in a large, deep saucepan until the salt and sugar have dissolved. Put over a high heat until your brine comes to the boil, then remove from the heat and allow to cool before refrigerating overnight. The next day, place your brisket in a large non-reactive tub or deep tray that fits the brisket snugly.

↓

2

Using a brining syringe, inject the brine into the centre of the brisket in a 2.5 cm (1 inch) grid all over the entire brisket. The meat will change in colour from a light pink to a dark maroon as you do this. Pour any remaining brine over the meat so it's completely submerged (you may need to weigh it down). Refrigerate for 3 days.

3
DRYING & SMOKING

Remove the brisket from the brine, pat it dry, then place on a wire rack over a tray. Put in the fridge, uncovered, and leave to dry for at least 12 hours.

Once dry, cold smoke the brisket (see page 138) for 1½ hours. Change the charcoal and wood chips every 30 minutes.

4
COOKING

Preheat your oven to 100°C (200°F/Gas ½). Place the brisket on a wire rack in a deep roasting tin and cover with baking paper and a double layer of foil. Poke four small holes through the top of the foil. Bake for 12–14 hours, or until the meat is just holding but has the texture of corned beef.

5

Increase the oven temperature to 200°C (400°F/Gas 6). Move the brisket and the rack to a clean, deep roasting tin. Brush lightly with blended oil and cook for 20 minutes, or until it has some nice colour. Remove, slice and serve.

↓

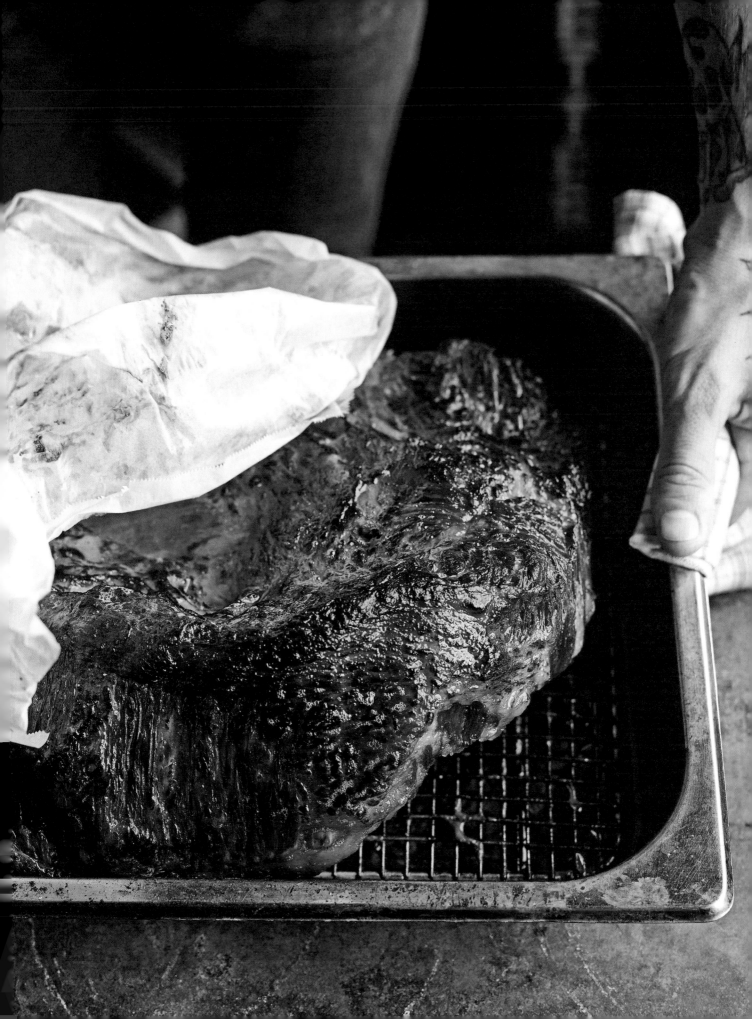

SMOKED FISH

When you are selecting fish for curing and smoking, it's so important to find the freshest fish you can because it's going to be out of the fridge for quite a long time, so it can get even stronger and 'fishier' if it's not really fresh in the first place. This process works for all types of fish, but we think the flavour profile of oily, fatty fish, like mackerel, works best. These varieties also tend to hold up better than more delicate fish in the brining and smoking process.

500–800 g (1 lb 2 oz–1 lb 12 oz) whole
    mackerel (or other oily fish)
or
4 × 150–200 g (5½–7 oz) mackerel
    fillets (or other fish), skin on

BRINE

The quantities of water, salt and brown sugar you'll need depend on whether you're preparing whole fish or fillets. Check the smoking chart (pgs 138–139) for guidance.

=== 1 ===
PREPARING WHOLE FISH

Scale if necessary, then gut and remove the gills.

=== 2 ===

Use a spoon to remove the blood-line that runs along the spine (this can give the fish a metallic taste). Rinse in ice-cold water then pat dry. If you're smoking the fish whole, you can put it right into the brine now.

↓

↓

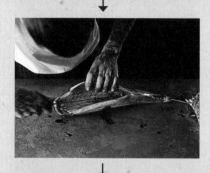

↓

↓

If preparing fillets, remove the head, cut along the spine and then above the ribs to get the fillets. Use the bones for guidance so you get two top loins and two belly fillets from each fish.

4
BRINING

Place the fish in a non-reactive container. Whisk all of the brine ingredients together in a large bowl until the salt and sugar have dissolved, then pour over the fish so it is fully submerged. Cover and store in the fridge for 2–3 days for whole fish, or 45–60 minutes for fillets. (Whole fish get longer than fillets because the brine has to penetrate the bones and skin.)

5
DRYING

Remove the fish from the brine and pat dry. If smoking whole fish, tie string around the tail of each fish and hang to dry over a tray in the fridge overnight so they maintain their nice shape and dry evenly. Fillets can be placed on a wire rack over a tray, skin side down, and dried in the fridge for 4–12 hours, or overnight if possible.

↓

↓

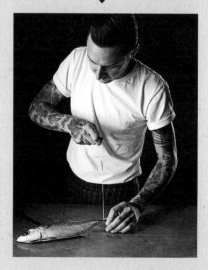

6

SMOKING

Hang the whole fish in the smoker so the flavours can penetrate evenly. Smoke on a low-medium smoke for 45–90 minutes (timings will depend on the size of the fish). Smoke the fillets, skin side down again, for 30–45 minutes on a low-medium smoke. Generally speaking, when the fish has taken on the smoke the flesh should have a yellowish tinge to it.

7

COOKING

After smoking, preheat the oven to 52°C (126°F). Cook whole fish for 25–30 minutes and fillets for 15–20 minutes, then remove from the oven and leave to cool. Store in an airtight container and keep in the fridge for up to 1 week.

NOTE:

If you plan to confit, steam, pan-fry or cook the fish in any way before serving, you can skip this last cooking step completely.

SMOKING CHART

We like to use the cold smoking method because it gives us more control over temperature and gives the product a more delicate finish. When we cold smoke, we use different types of wood chips depending on what's available. When starting your smoke, use a little charcoal to get the chips going. You want to produce plenty of smoke but no fire because that will alter the taste of the product, and the resin from burning wood is not nice.

Smoke is very personal; some people like a lot, some like a little. We don't smoke anything heavily, even if it is in the smoker for hours. We prefer a slower, gentle smoke.

Once the product is smoked to your liking, place it on a rack in the oven and cook it really slowly until the desired temperature is reached. This can sometimes take hours, or even overnight if you're working with a big piece of meat, but be patient because it's more than worth the effort.

	LEG HAM	BACON	BRISKET
PREP	1 × 3 kg (6 lb 12 oz) leg of ham (we use weaner pigs), excess fat and veins removed	1 × 3–4 kg (6 lb 12 oz–9 lb) pork belly, bone in, keep whole	1 × 2.5 kg (5 lb 8 oz) piece of wagyu brisket, keep whole
FOR THE BRINE	4 litres (140 fl oz) water 300 g (10½ oz) fine sea salt 325 g (11½ oz) brown sugar 40 g (1½ oz) sodium nitrate (see Glossary)	4 litres (140 fl oz) water 375 g (13 oz) fine sea salt 250 g (9 oz) brown sugar 30 g (1 oz) sodium nitrate (see Glossary)	4 litres (140 fl oz) water 350 g (12 oz) fine sea salt 90 g (3¼ oz) brown sugar 225 g (8 oz) caster (superfine) sugar 40 g (1½ oz) sodium nitrate (see Glossary) 60 g (2¼ oz) honey
BRINE TIME	3 weeks	10–12 days	3 days if injected (see page 132) 10 days if not injected
DRY TIME	12–24 hours	12–24 hours	12–24 hours
SMOKE TIME	3–5 hours low–medium	3–4 hours medium	1½ hours medium
COOKING TIME	70°C (158°F/Gas ¼) 4–7 hours, or until internal temp reaches 68°C (154°F)	90°C (195°F/Gas ½) 3 hours, or until internal temp reaches 68°C (154°F)	100°C (200°F/Gas ½) 12–14 hours

	WHOLE FISH	FISH FILLETS	OYSTERS
PREP	500–800 g (1 lb 2 oz–1 lb 12 oz) mackerel or other oily fish scale (if needed), gut and remove gills	150–200 g (5½–7 oz) fillets of mackerel or other oily fish, pin-boned	shucked and release
BRINE	1.25 litres (44 fl oz) water 65 g (2⅓ oz) salt 100 g (3½ oz) brown sugar	750 ml (26 fl oz) water 30 g (1 oz) salt 50 g (1¾ oz) brown sugar	X
BRINE TIME	2–3 days	45 minutes–1 hour	X
DRY TIME	8–12 hours	4–12 hours	X
SMOKE TIME	45 minutes–1½ hours low–medium	30–45 minutes low–medium	15–20 minutes high
COOKING TIME	52–54°C (126–129°F) 25–30 minutes	52–54°C (126–129°F) 15–20 minutes	120°C (235°F/Gas ½) 10 minutes

	CHICKEN WINGS	BUTTER/CHEESE	NUTS
PREP	2 kg (4 lb 8 oz) chicken wings, wing joints split and wing tips removed	sliced 1 cm (½ inch) thick	soaked in water or lightly spiced brine
BRINE	1 litre (35 fl oz) water 45 g (1¾ oz) salt 60 g (2¼ oz) brown sugar	X	water to cover
BRINE TIME	4 hours	X	soak for 30 minutes
DRY TIME	8–12 hours	X	1–2 hours
SMOKE TIME	2 hours medium–high	20 minutes medium–high	45 minutes–1 hour medium–high
COOKING TIME	steam for 20 minutes deep-fry to serve	X	roast at 160°C (315°F/Gas 2–3) for 6 minutes. Toast as needed

PORTEÑO

We've eaten some of the best meals of our lives at Elvis's folks' place. Weekend after weekend we'd sit around their garage while his old man built a cracking barbie and served up plate after plate of beautifully cooked meat. And the whole time we'd be thinking, 'This is the greatest Sunday ever. Imagine if we could turn this experience into a restaurant.' And that's how the whole idea for Porteño started; we wanted to share a piece of that garage with everyone.

We knew right from the beginning that we wanted to cook whole animals over fire right there in the restaurant. We also wanted as much as possible coming off a charcoal grill. When it came to the eating, we didn't want people feeling they had to be too prim and proper in the way they went about things — we prefer dishes in the middle of the table, so everyone can share.

There was only ever one location we wanted to open Porteño and that was the building that had housed the legendary Greek restaurant, Dimitri's, on Cleveland Street in Surry Hills. It's a strange and wonderful building with heaps of character (as well as leaks and cold spots here and there).

Dimitri's had been an institution since the late '60s and by the '80s had become a favourite spot for politicians, businessmen and shady characters doing business lunches. It had been closed for about seven years by the time we came along, and its glory days were well and truly behind it.

We all thought, 'Oh yeah, we'll come in and fix it up. Easy.' But it wasn't; it was the pits! There was a hole in the roof, uneaten food on the bench and loads of structural problems not to mention a huge fountain feature smack bang in the middle of the floor, which was killer to get out. And of course there were a few Greek statues thrown in for good measure.

Needless to say, it took us a year and a half to open the doors, and getting to that point totally crushed us. We were working 12-hour days six days a week at Bodega, Ben was a new dad, and we were spending every free second at Porteño knocking down walls. We had no money and we were so tired.

Two days before we opened we all stood around in amazement thinking, 'We did it!' That's when Joe says, 'You reckon it's gonna work?' We all looked at each other and laughed for about five minutes — we'd never stopped to think about what everyone else would think, we'd just built the place we'd always wanted to go to. Luckily for all of us, people loved it.

In the past six years we've gone from a kitchen of three at Bodega to 70 people all up across the two restaurants. It's been a learning curve, but it's all been worth it.

BEETROOT SALAD

Serves 8

STUFFED OLIVES

200 g (7 oz) green Sicilian olives
blended oil (95% canola + 5% extra
  virgin)
6 long red chillies

GARLIC CONFIT

2 garlic bulbs
200 ml (7 fl oz) extra virgin olive oil

BEETROOT SALAD

2 heads of witlof (chicory)
12 baby golden beetroot (beets),
  trimmed
12 baby purple beetroot (beets),
  trimmed
600 g (1 lb 5 oz) rock salt
200 g (7 oz) feta cheese (see
  pgs 106–110)
20 ml (½ fl oz) balsamic vinegar
fine sea salt and freshly ground black
  pepper
135 g (4¾ oz) stuffed olives (see above)
100 g (3½ oz) smoked pecans
  (see smoking chart pg 139)
300 g (10½ oz) watercress, picked
extra virgin olive oil

STUFFED OLIVES

Carefully pit the olives so you can stuff them later. If they're
too hard, warm them over a low heat in a small saucepan
with enough blended oil to cover them. Cook gently for about
15–20 minutes, or just enough to soften them. Keep the
oil to store the olives in later.

Get your barbecue going (see page 212) and barbecue the
chillies until blackened all over, then place in a bowl, cover
with plastic wrap and leave to steam and cool. Once cool
enough to handle, peel, deseed and chop them.
Stuff the chillies inside the olives then place them in a jar and
pour in enough of their cooking oil to cover them completely.
Seal and store in the fridge for up to 1 month.

GARLIC CONFIT

Place the garlic bulbs directly onto the hot coals of the
barbecue, turning occasionally until black on the outside
(this should take about 5–8 minutes). Place the charred bulbs
in a bowl, cover with plastic wrap and leave to steam and cool.

Once cool enough to handle, peel away the charred garlic
skins and retrieve each clove, carefully placing them in a small
saucepan with the extra virgin olive oil. Place over a very low
heat and gently cook for about 5 minutes, or until soft. Remove
the pan from the heat and keep the garlic in the oil until ready
to dish up.

BEETROOT SALAD

Halve the witlofs by cutting down the centre of each head.
Grill over the hot coals for about 5–10 minutes, or until dark
all over. Remove from the heat, place in a bowl and cover with
plastic wrap.

Preheat the oven to 180°C (350°F/Gas 4) and place the
beetroot on a bed of rock salt in a roasting tin, cover with
foil and place in the oven for 25–30 minutes, or until cooked
(when a skewer passes through them easily).

Remove the beetroot, allow to cool for 10 minutes then
pull off the foil. Remove and discard the stems and peel the
beetroot while they're still warm, keeping the two colours in
separate bowls. Their skins should slip off with ease.

Remove the cooled witlof core with a knife, trying to keep it in one piece, then discard it.

Place the witlof on a serving platter, spreading out their leaves, then spoon the feta cheese over them in a few spots.

Dress the purple beetroot with balsamic vinegar and season with salt and pepper. Season the golden beetroot with salt and pepper. Slice or cut some of the larger beets into wedges if you like, then scatter them around the platter with the olives and pecans.

Carefully remove the confit garlic from the oil and place around the platter. Quickly dress the watercress with some extra virgin olive oil, salt and pepper, then place it over the beetroot and finish with a final crack of black pepper.

SMOKED MACKEREL, POTATO & PALM HEART SALAD Serves 8

2 waxy potatoes such
   as royal blue or desiree
2 mackerels, filleted & cold smoked
   (see smoking chart pg 139)
4 preserved palm hearts in brine,
   drained
4 stalks of pickled celery (see
   pg 275) and 4 tablespoons
   of their pickling liquor
2 French shallots
1 tablespoon lemon juice
125 ml (4 fl oz) extra virgin olive oil
2 teaspoons river salt flakes
1 avocado
4 tablespoons salsa golf (see
   pg 274)
a few sprigs of picked dill, for garnish
a few celery leaves, for garnish
8 chives, cut into batons

Place the potatoes in a small deep saucepan, cover with cold water and bring to the boil over a medium heat. Gently cook them for 15–20 minutes, then turn off the heat and leave them to stand in the cooling water for about 15 minutes.

Torch the skin side of each smoked fish fillet using a kitchen blowtorch on a high flame. Work up and down the fillet until you achieve a nice, consistent char then set aside, skin side up.

Slice the palm hearts into rounds, finely slice the celery and French shallots, and then combine them in a bowl with the pickling liquor, lemon juice, extra virgin olive oil and salt.

Go back and torch the other side of the fish lightly, for a few seconds only, to cook them perfectly.

Halve, stone, peel and slice the avocado, and peel and slice the warm potatoes. Arrange them on serving plates to form a base, then place the mackerel on top. Spoon over the dressed vegetables then drizzle over any dressing from the bowl.

Finish with spoonfuls of salsa golf and garnish generously with dill, celery leaves and chives.

JARRED OCTOPUS

Serves 8

8 octopus (about 165 g/5¾ oz each)

1 garlic bulb, cloves separated, peeled
    and sliced

2 × 200 g (7 oz) dried, cured chorizo
    sausages from a deli, cut into 1 cm
    (½ inch) slices

8 French shallots, peeled
    and halved

2 teaspoons dried chilli flakes

400–500 ml (14–17 fl oz) extra virgin
    olive oil

To clean each octopus, slice horizontally beneath the eyes, push the beak out from between the tentacles and discard it.

Now make an incision from the top of the head and slice down the back, this will allow you to turn the flesh inside out. Use a sharp knife to ease away the innards attached to the meat. Slice horizontally above the eyes and discard them. Gently wash the tentacles and the flesh from the head.

Place the tentacles on a grill placed directly over the flames of a wood fire or a gas flame (make sure you are wearing flame-retardant gloves and use long-handled tongs). Char the tentacles evenly for about 30 seconds then remove from the heat.

Repeat the process with the heads. You want them charred and blackened on the outside but not burnt to a crisp. The octopus should still be raw inside.

Slice the cooked tentacles and heads into bite-sized pieces about 2.5 cm (1 inch).

Evenly layer the octopus, sliced garlic, chorizo and shallot, into eight 125 ml (4 fl oz) capacity sterilised jars, packing everything in tightly and adding a good pinch of chilli flakes to each jar. Pour in enough extra virgin olive oil to cover everything completely, then seal your jars tightly.

Preheat a combination oven with a steam function to 100°C (200°F/Gas ½) and cook the octopus jars on a steamer tray at full steam for 1½ hours. If you don't have a combi oven, steam in a large stovetop steamer for the same amount of time (topping up the water as necessary).

Set aside to cool slightly for 15 minutes, or until warm to the touch then serve the jars with steamed potato and bitter leaves like witlof (chicory) or radicchio and thinly sliced shallot to garnish. Alternatively, you can cool the jars to room temperature and refrigerate until needed. They'll keep for up to 1 week unopened and you can just reheat them by steaming at the same setting as before for 15 minutes.

BARBECUED MARROW & LAMB TARTARE WITH FLATBREAD Serves 8

BEEF SHIN

4 × 12 cm (4½ inch) pieces of beef shin, halved lengthways (ask your butcher to do this for you)
8 spring onions (scallions)
100 ml (3½ fl oz) chimichurri (see pg 273)

GRILLED CHEWY FLATBREAD

200 ml (7 fl oz) lukewarm water
1 tablespoon extra virgin olive oil
1 teaspoon dried yeast
1 teaspoon caster (superfine) sugar
1 teaspoon fine sea salt
360 g (12¾ oz) plain (all-purpose) flour

LAMB TARTARE

8 long red chillies
750 g (1 lb 10 oz) lamb leg meat, trimmed of all sinew and fat, diced
4 French shallots, diced
5 tablespoons chopped flat-leaf (Italian) parsley
3 tablespoons chopped mint
1½ teaspoons tomato paste (concentrated purée)
1½ teaspoons ground allspice
1½ teaspoons ground dried chilli
1½ teaspoons ground cinnamon
1½ teaspoons sweet smoked paprika
3 teaspoons fine sea salt
3 teaspoons freshly ground black pepper
3 tablespoons hot English mustard
80 ml (2½ fl oz) extra virgin olive oil

BEEF SHIN

Place the beef shins in a bowl of icy, salted water. Cover, then refrigerate and leave to soak for 6 hours, or overnight. This will help to get rid of the blood. Remove from the water and pat dry.

GRILLED CHEWY FLATBREAD

Mix the water, extra virgin olive oil, yeast, sugar and salt together in a bowl. Leave for 30 minutes, or until it starts to bubble.

Place the flour in a wide bowl. Create a well in the middle and add the water mixture to the flour, whisking slowly and bringing in the flour from the side. Once thick, use your hands to bring it all together then knead for 5–10 minutes until elastic.

Place in a lightly oiled bowl, cover with plastic wrap and leave in a warm place to prove for 2 hours.

After that, knock the dough back and return it to the bowl, covered, to prove for another 30 minutes.

LAMB TARTARE

Get a barbecue going (see page 212) and cook the chillies directly over the hot coals, turning occasionally, until charred all over. Remove them to a bowl, cover with plastic wrap and leave to steam. Once cool enough to handle, peel and discard the stalks, skins and seeds then finely chop.

Combine the chillies and the rest of the ingredients (except the English mustard and extra virgin olive oil) in a large bowl and refrigerate for 1 hour.

TO SERVE

When nearly ready to serve, divide the dough for your flatbreads into eight balls and let them rest on a tray for 5 minutes. Roll the dough balls into rough oval shapes about 3 mm (⅛ inch) thick. Grill over the hot coals for 40 seconds, then turn and cook for 20 seconds more, until charred.

Put the tartare through a mincer with a 5 mm (¼ inch) attachment. Pass it through a second time with an ice cube in each handful so the meat stays cold.

Taste and adjust the seasoning, add the English mustard and the extra virgin olive oil then put the tartare in the fridge while you finish the beef shins.

Grill the spring onions over the hot coals then slice them and fold through the chimichurri. Cook the beef shins over the hot coals, cut side up, for 5 minutes, or until the bones are hot. Colour up the marrow by grilling them under a salamander or preheated oven grill (broiler).

Drizzle the chimichurri all over the grilled beef shin and serve with the cold lamb tartare and grilled flatbreads.

BRUSSELS SPROUTS

Serves 8

The sprouts on our menu are successful because no one expects them to be good. You have to convince people to order the dish and go, 'Honestly, if you don't like them you can throw them at me.' People fight for them — there's never a bowl that comes back to the kitchen. And everyone wants to tell you their traumatic story about how they needed counselling because of the brussels sprouts they had when they were young. Admittedly, this dish has a mix of weird ingredients, but when they're all together it's a pretty unique dressing. And that's a big part of the reason why these are so delicious. If you don't have a deep-fryer, you can just heat a couple of litres of oil in a really deep pot. Just know that it's quite dangerous, as the sprouts really tend to spit once they hit the oil. Even Elvis still nails himself doing this dish. You can roast them, or heat them in a pan if you don't want to deep-fry them. But we reckon you should live on the edge. Just don't burn your house down.

BRUSSELS SPROUTS

75 g (2¾ oz) dried green lentils

1 kg (2 lb 4 oz) brussels sprouts (don't wash them! This is important.)

cottonseed oil, for deep-frying

river salt flakes

40 g (1½ oz) mint, leaves picked

40 g (1½ oz) flat-leaf (Italian) parsley, leaves picked

DRESSING

1 tablespoon hot English mustard

50 ml (1½ fl oz) vincotto

100 ml (3½ fl oz) extra virgin olive oil

a pinch of fine sea salt and freshly ground black pepper

Cook the lentils in simmering water for 8–10 minutes, or until just tender, then drain and set aside.

Whisk together all of the dressing ingredients.

Trim the ends of the brussels sprouts and remove any outer leaves. Wipe them with a dry cloth if you need to remove any dirt, but don't wash them! (Any extra water will make them even more volatile when you deep-fry them in the hot oil.)

Cut them in half lengthways then fill a large, deep heavy-based saucepan a third full (no more) with the cottonseed oil. Heat it to 180°C (350°F) then deep-fry the brussels sprouts in batches until they're golden and crispy (stand back! They will spit as they fry).

Drain them on paper towel then place in a large bowl and season with the river salt flakes. Add the dressing, lentils, mint and parsley then toss to coat and suckemdown!

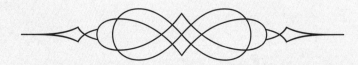

FENNEL SALAD

Serves 8

BOOZY APRICOTS

150 ml (5 fl oz) Amontillado sherry

3 tablespoons honey

100 ml (3½ fl oz) water

fine sea salt

100 g (3½ oz) dried apricots

FENNEL SALAD

100 g (3½ oz) pitted kalamata olives
    in brine

2 teaspoons fennel seeds

4 fennel bulbs

50 g (1¾ oz) dill, picked

50 ml (1½ fl oz) chardonnay vinegar

60 ml (2 fl oz) extra virgin olive oil

BOOZY APRICOTS

Whisk the sherry, honey and water in a large bowl. The combination should be sweet and thick, so adjust to taste with honey and sherry. Add a pinch of salt, but remember that the olives will also be salty; you don't want to over season at this stage.

Soak your apricots in this liquid for at least 24 hours at room temperature, then keep in the fridge until ready to use (this will keep in the fridge for up to 3 months).

FENNEL SALAD

Drain the kalamata olives from their brine, pat dry with paper towel and leave for 4 hours before layering evenly in a dehydrator set at 50°C (122°F) for 12 hours. If you don't have a dehydrator, spread the olives out on a baking tray and dry in the oven at 140°C (275°F/Gas 1) for 2 hours until semi-dried.

Slice the soaked apricots into strips and keep their liquid to dress the salad with later.

Toast your fennel seeds in a small, dry frying pan over the lowest heat for a few minutes, tossing occasionally. This will release the natural oils in the seeds and increase their flavour and aroma. A slight smokiness will come off the seeds when they're a little darker and ready to use. Transfer to a bowl to cool.

Slice the base off each fennel bulb, remove the fibrous outer leaves then thinly slice the bulbs and place in a large bowl. Add the dill, fennel seeds, dehydrated olives, vinegar and extra virgin olive oil. Add a few spoonfuls of the sliced apricots and their liquid. Toss to coat, then taste and adjust with a little more of the liquid if you like before serving.

BARBECUED PEPPERS & EGGPLANTS

Serves 8

We like to barbecue our vegetables when the coals have reached their highest heat (see page 212).

Cook the capsicums on a grill placed quite low over the coals until their skins turn black all over. Once this has happened, transfer them to a large bowl and cover with plastic wrap. Steaming them for a few minutes like this makes it easier to remove the skins. Once they have cooled a little, remove all their skin and seeds, dress them heavily with some extra virgin olive oil, a few pinches of salt and the sliced garlic.

The same principle applies to barbecuing eggplant, but you need to make sure you prick the skins with a fork before cooking otherwise they will explode (not good). Cook them on a grill placed quite low over the coals, for around 10 minutes on each side, ensuring the skins burn; this adds a smoky flavour. Remove from the barbecue then rest on a wire rack until cool enough to handle.

To remove the flesh, slice the tops off the eggplants then split them in half lengthways. Use a spoon to scoop out the flesh and dress with extra virgin olive oil and salt. Serve the eggplant and capsicums together on a platter.

8 red bullhorn capsicums (peppers)
extra virgin olive oil
fine sea salt
2 garlic cloves, thinly sliced
4 eggplants (aubergines)

POLENTA & BARBECUED RADICCHIO WITH ANCHOVY & ROSEMARY POUND Serves 8

ANCHOVY & ROSEMARY POUND

10 g (¼ oz) rosemary leaves

12 brown anchovy fillets in oil

juice of 1 lemon

100 ml (3½ fl oz) extra virgin olive oil

POLENTA & RADICCHIO

2 heads of treviso radicchio

1 litre (35 fl oz) milk

250 g (9 oz) fine white polenta (cornmeal)

extra virgin olive oil

fine sea salt

80 g (2¾ oz) unsalted butter, diced

100 g (3½ oz) provolone dolce cheese, coarsely grated

ANCHOVY & ROSEMARY POUND

Place the rosemary in a mortar and pound to a paste with the pestle. Add the anchovies and pound again until you have an even paste.

Drizzle in the lemon juice and extra virgin olive oil, whisk until combined then set aside until ready to use.

POLENTA & RADICCHIO

Trim the ends of the radicchio cores, remove any ragged outer leaves and quarter lengthways.

Heat the milk in a medium saucepan over a high heat until it's just about to boil, then whisk in the polenta and turn the heat down to low.

Stir continuously for the first 5 minutes then frequently from that point on, adding splashes of water as needed when it gets too thick or starts sticking. (Depending on the brand of polenta it could take up to 600 ml/21 fl oz of water.) Cook for 45–60 minutes, or until thick, smooth and cooked.

When the polenta is about 10 minutes away from being perfect, lightly drizzle the radicchio with extra virgin olive oil and a few pinches of salt. Preheat a grill pan over a high heat, or get the barbecue good and hot, then cook them, sliced side down, for 2–3 minutes, turning to grill them evenly all over.

Transfer the grilled radicchio to a bowl, cover with plastic wrap and leave to steam for 5 minutes.

Stir the butter and the provolone through the polenta so they melt in, then season to taste with salt and serve straight away.

Pour the polenta onto two serving platters, arrange the grilled radicchio on top then finish by spooning over the anchovy and rosemary pound.

CAULIFLOWER, CHICKPEA & SILVERBEET SALAD Serves 8

Drain the soaked chickpeas then put them in a medium saucepan, cover well with cold, salted water and bring to the boil over a high heat. Once boiling, reduce the heat and simmer until tender then drain and put aside.

Slice the garlic as thinly as you possibly can then cook it in the extra virgin olive oil in a small saucepan over a medium heat until the garlic is golden brown and crisp. Strain the garlic, drain on paper towel and reserve the cooking oil.

Trim the white stems from each leaf of silverbeet so you are left with two long pieces of leaf (discard the stems). Steam the leaves for 3 minutes.

Fill a large, deep heavy-based saucepan a third full (no more) with oil. Heat it to 180°C (350°F) then deep-fry the cauliflower florets in batches for 3–4 minutes, or until dark golden brown. Drain them on paper towel and season heavily with salt and pepper.

Heat 150 ml (5 fl oz) of the reserved garlic oil in a large heavy-based frying pan over a medium–high heat. Add the cumin seeds, then the silverbeet, chickpeas, crisp cauliflower and lemon juice and cook until warmed through.

Transfer to a serving dish, sprinkle over the garlic chips and serve.

200 g (7 oz) dried chickpeas, soaked in cold water overnight
4 garlic cloves
200 ml (7 fl oz) extra virgin olive oil
2 kg (4 lb 8 oz/2 bunches) silverbeet (Swiss chard)
cottonseed oil, for deep-frying
1 head of cauliflower, cut into small florets, stem discarded
fine sea salt and freshly ground black pepper
1 tablespoon cumin seeds
juice of 1 lemon

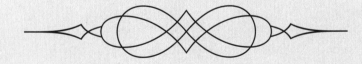

TOMATO & ONION SALAD

Serves 8

This is our favourite salad. We like to keep it really simple, and quite vinegary. It's our salad of choice when we're eating a steak.

6 oxheart tomatoes
1 white onion
fine sea salt
sherry vinegar
extra virgin olive oil
dried oregano

Cut the tomatoes into big rough wedges and slice the white onion thinly.

Arrange on a platter and season with salt.

Dress with drizzles of sherry vinegar and extra virgin olive oil, to taste.

Sprinkle over a pinch of dried oregano and serve.

THE PORTEÑO PAVLOVA

Serves 8

This is based on a Uruguayan dessert of sponge, tinned fruit, meringue, cream and peanuts. At Porteño we make it with mango, but we poach it to simulate the tinned stuff. You could definitely use tinned mango if you didn't want to poach it yourself, in fact we'd recommend it. You soak the sponge in the fruit syrup, and then add the salty peanuts, cream and meringue. In South America it usually comes wrapped up in greaseproof paper. You unwrap it, put your face in and just motorboat it. But it's totally seasonal so you can use any fruit you like. Every celebration, Elvis's mum makes the cake version of this. It's just layers of sponge and caramel and more sponge and then fruit and nuts. That's his favourite thing in the world to eat: cold cake straight out of the fridge from the night before.

MERINGUES (SEE NOTE)

105 g (3½ oz) egg whites

120 g (4¼ oz) caster (superfine) sugar

2 teaspoons potato starch

½ teaspoon white vinegar

> NOTE: MAKE THE MERINGUES
> IN ADVANCE TO FREE UP YOUR
> OVEN FOR THE SPONGE.

SPONGE

4 eggs

120 g (4¼ oz) caster (superfine) sugar

100 g (3½ oz) plain (all-purpose)
  flour, sifted

20 g (¾ oz) almond meal

MANGOES

4 mangoes

200 g (7 oz) caster (superfine) sugar

200 ml (7 fl oz) water

juice of 1 lime

45 ml (1½ fl oz) dark rum

DIPLOMAT

125 g (4½ oz) chilled crème pâtissière
  (see pgs 184–185 — but leave out
  the tequila!)

400 g (14 oz) cream (45% fat)

TO SERVE

250 g (9 oz) dulce de leche

8 passionfruit, halved and pulp
  scooped out

150 g (5½ oz) salted peanuts
  (see pgs 43–45)

MERINGUES

Preheat the oven to 110°C (225°F/Gas ½). Whisk your egg whites using an electric mixer (we use old egg whites at room temperature for the best result). Once they start to peak, add half your sugar and keep whisking for a few minutes. Add the remaining sugar and whisk for a further 5 minutes, or until stiff peaks form. Add the potato starch and vinegar, and whisk for a further 5 minutes until smooth and glossy.

Line a baking tray with baking paper then scoop four big kitchen spoonfuls of the mixture onto the tray, leaving a minimum of 2.5 cm (1 inch) between them.

Bake for 45–60 minutes until still very slightly soft to the touch and starting to colour. Turn off the oven and leave the tray in there with the door ajar until the meringues have completely cooled. Once cool, they can be stored in an airtight container for up to 4 days.

SPONGE

Whisk the eggs and sugar using an electric mixer for about 5 minutes, or until very fluffy. Transfer the mix into a large bowl and carefully fold in the sifted flour then the almond meal using a rubber spatula.

Line a 15 × 20 cm (6 × 8 inch) baking tray that's about 6 cm (2½ inches) deep with baking paper. Pour the sponge mixture into the tray, smooth out the top then tightly wrap the entire tray with plastic wrap so it's airtight. Preheat a combination oven with a steam function to 100°C (200°F/Gas ½) and steam at full steam for 17–20 minutes. Once out, quickly remove the wrap, being careful not to burn yourself, and leave to cool.

Alternatively, you could bake the sponge in a buttered, floured and lined baking tray at 170°C (325°F/Gas 3) for 30 minutes.

MANGOES

Peel the mangoes with a sharp knife, removing the two cheeks from either side of the stone and carving off any other flesh. Slice each cheek lengthways into four segments and put in a container.

Place the mango stones in a large saucepan with the sugar and water and bring to the boil over a medium heat. Once boiling, turn down and simmer for about 1 minute then remove from the heat and allow to stand for 5 minutes. Strain the mango syrup through a fine sieve into a jug.

Add the lime juice and rum to the warm syrup, stir, then immediately pour all over the mangoes. Allow to cool down in the refrigerator.

DIPLOMAT

Whisk the crème pâtissière in a large bowl until smooth.

Slowly fold the cream into the crème pâtissière. Add a little at a time so you use it up in around four to six goes. This will give you a nice velvety cream finish that will really hold up in the dessert.

TO SERVE

Drain the mango from its syrup. Break the sponge into chunks and drizzle a generous amount of the mango syrup all over so it is really moist.

Gently smash the meringues into rough chunks. Divide these elements evenly between your serving plates then add spoonfuls of diplomat, dulce de leche and passionfruit pulp around the plates. Top with a scattering of peanuts and serve.

CINNAMON-DOUGH TART WITH FIGS, MUSCAT ICE CREAM & BLUE CHEESE CREAM

Makes 8

MUSCAT ICE CREAM
650 ml (22½ fl oz) milk
150 ml (5 fl oz) cream (35% fat)
60 g (2¼ oz) skim milk powder
150 g (5½ oz) liquid glucose
  (see Glossary)
210 g (7½ oz) caster (superfine)
  sugar
5 egg yolks
100 ml (3½ fl oz) sun-dried muscat
  (sweet Argentinean wine)

BLUE CHEESE CREAM
500 ml (17 fl oz) cream (35% fat)
90 g (3¼ oz) caster (superfine) sugar
90 g (3¼ oz) egg yolks
6 g (⅕ oz) leaf gelatine
  (see Glossary)
125 g (4½ oz) soft blue cheese
  (gorgonzola dolce), chopped

CINNAMON PASTRY
3 eggs
300 g (10½ oz) unsalted butter,
  softened
125 g (4½ oz) caster (superfine)
  sugar
20 ml (½ fl oz) dark rum
50 g (1¾ oz) almond meal
3 teaspoons ground cinnamon
325 g (11½ oz) plain (all-purpose)
  flour, plus extra for dusting
¼ teaspoon baking powder
uncooked rice, for blind baking

TO SERVE
8 fresh figs, sliced
1 nutmeg, for grating

MUSCAT ICE CREAM
Place all the ingredients, except the muscat, in a deep saucepan and blitz really well using a hand-held stick blender.

Place the saucepan over a medium heat, stir constantly and bring up to 83°C (181°F).

Strain through a fine sieve into a container, refrigerate until chilled then add the muscat and stir through. Cover and leave overnight in the refrigerator.

The next day, blitz again using the hand-held stick blender, then churn in an ice-cream machine, following the manufacturer's instructions. Freeze at -18°C (-0.4°F) until needed.

BLUE CHEESE CREAM
Combine the cream and 60 g (2¼ oz) of the sugar in a medium heavy-based saucepan and bring to the boil.

Whisk the egg yolks and remaining sugar together until pale and smooth. Once the cream has boiled, pour a small amount onto the egg mixture and whisk to combine. Whisk the egg mixture into the rest of the cream.

Place the saucepan over a medium heat. Cook, stirring continuously with a wooden spoon, until it reaches 83°C (181°F) then remove from the heat and set aside. Place the gelatine leaves in cold water and set aside to soften.

Place the cheese in a heatproof bowl and sit over a saucepan of just simmering water. Make sure the water doesn't touch the bottom of the bowl. Stir occasionally until just melted then mix into the cream mixture and strain. Squeeze any excess water from the gelatine then add it to the mixture and stir to dissolve. Set aside to cool slightly, stirring occasionally as it cools to prevent a skin forming. Place some plastic wrap on top so it's in contact with the cream and chill in the fridge overnight.

The next day, place in an electric mixer bowl and whisk on high until smooth and thick. But be careful not to over whisk. Spoon into a piping (icing) bag with a star nozzle and refrigerate for 2–4 hours. The mixture will firm up even more in the piping bag as it chills.

CINNAMON PASTRY

Cook the eggs in boiling water for 10 minutes then place them in ice water. Once cold, peel the eggs and discard the whites. Pass the yolks through a fine sieve and set aside.

Cream the butter and sugar together using an electric mixer until pale and creamy. Add the egg yolks and rum and continue to mix, making sure you scrape the sides of the bowl with a spatula as you go. Mix on a slow setting and gradually add in the dry ingredients.

When all the ingredients are combined, turn the dough out onto a floured work surface. Bring together with your hands then wrap in plastic wrap and chill in the refrigerator for 1 hour.

Cut the dough into eight pieces and roll out one piece at a time on a floured work surface until it is 2–3 mm (⅛ inch) thick.

Working carefully (the pastry is quite delicate), place the pastry into eight round tart tins about 10 cm (4 inches) in diameter and 2.5 cm (1 inch) deep. Make sure the pastry is pressed firmly into the base and side of the tins. Using a knife, trim off any excess pastry, arrange the tart tins on a tray and refrigerate for 30 minutes.

Preheat the oven to 160°C (315°F/Gas 2–3). Remove the tart cases from the refrigerator, line each one with a double layer of plastic wrap then fill them with uncooked rice. Twist the plastic wrap to seal.

Blind bake for 15 minutes, then remove the rice and bake for another 5–10 minutes, or until the pastry is golden. Leave to cool.

TO SERVE

Lay the slices of figs in the tart shells and top with a scoop of the ice cream. Pipe the blue cheese cream on top to cover the ice cream then finely grate over some nutmeg and serve right away.

BURNT MILK CUSTARD, CHOCOLATE ICE CREAM & ORANGE PURÉE Serves 8

CHOCOLATE ICE CREAM
500 ml (17 fl oz) milk
35 g (1¼ oz) skim milk powder
25 g (1 oz) trimoline (invert sugar
 syrup) (see Glossary)
100 g (3½ oz) dextrose
 (see Glossary)
35 g (1¼ oz) caster (superfine) sugar
165 ml (5¼ fl oz) cream (35% fat)
60 g (2¼ oz) unsweetened cocoa
 powder, sifted
35 g (1¼ oz) dark chocolate
 (64% cocoa solids), chopped
85 ml (2¾ fl oz) Jack Daniel's
 whiskey (or the equivalent of
 10% of your total ice-cream
 mixture)

BURNT MILK BASE
625 ml (21½ fl oz) milk
425 g (15 oz) caster (superfine) sugar
4 medium-sized charcoals,
 red hot

BURNT MILK CUSTARD
500 ml (17 fl oz) burnt milk base
 (see above)
25 egg yolks
500 ml (17 fl oz) cream (35% fat)

ORANGE PURÉE
3 oranges (see note on pg 180)
1 kg (2 lb 4 oz) caster (superfine)
 sugar
1 litre (35 fl oz) cold water

SWEET ROSEMARY POPCORN
30 ml (1 fl oz) vegetable oil
50 g (1¾ oz) popping corn
150 g (5½ oz) caster (superfine)
 sugar
15 ml (½ fl oz) water
1¼ tablespoons very finely
 chopped rosemary leaves
¼ teaspoon fine sea salt

TO SERVE
110 g (3¾ oz) caster
 (superfine) sugar

CHOCOLATE ICE CREAM
Place all the ingredients (except the dark chocolate and Jack Daniel's) in a deep saucepan. Mix really well using a hand-held stick blender.

Place the saucepan over a medium heat, stir constantly and heat to 83°C (181°F). Put the chopped chocolate into a heatproof bowl.

Pour the hot mixture over the chocolate and stir gently until the chocolate has melted.

Strain into a container, then cover and refrigerate for 24 hours for the flavours to mature.

Add the Jack Daniel's and mix with a hand-held stick blender then churn in an ice-cream machine, following the manufacturer's instructions. Freeze at -18°C (-0.4°F) until needed.

BURNT MILK BASE
Heat your milk in a small saucepan over a medium heat until hot.

Heat the sugar in a separate small, deep heavy-based saucepan over a low–medium heat.

Very carefully, add the pieces of red-hot charcoal to the sugar pan and gently stir with an old wooden spoon. Don't stir hard. Continually turn the coals as if you were trying to put them out with the sugar, and place the pan over the heat as necessary until the sugar is melted.

Slowly add the hot milk to the melted sugar, but do not stir until all of the milk is incorporated then slowly stir to combine.

Carefully strain into a bowl through a fine sieve then through a piece of muslin (cheesecloth) or a coffee filter. Cool to room temperature then put in the fridge to chill.

BURNT MILK CUSTARD

Preheat the oven to 140°C (275°F/Gas 1).

Whisk all of the ingredients together really well then pour into an ovenproof dish, about 20 × 25 cm (8 × 10 inches) and 6 cm (2½ inches) deep. Cover with foil and prick a few holes in the top.

Place the dish in a roasting tin and pour enough hot water into the tin to come halfway up the sides of the dish. Bake for 60–80 minutes, or until just set. Remove from the oven, cool to room temperature then chill in the fridge.

ORANGE PURÉE

Put the oranges in a medium saucepan, cover with cold water and bring to the boil over a medium heat. Once boiling, change the water and repeat the process five more times.

Meanwhile, mix the sugar with the litre of water in a medium heavy-based saucepan.

Carefully remove the oranges from their cooking water and add them to the sugar mixture. Bring to the boil over a medium heat then turn down the heat and simmer gently until the liquid has reduced by half, and the oranges take on a candied appearance. The skin should be translucent and shiny and the liquid should be thick. Don't be tempted to touch or taste anything from the pan at this point, it will be beyond hot.

Remove the pan from the heat. Carefully spoon out the oranges and allow them to cool before halving and deseeding.

Place the oranges and a little of their cooking syrup in a blender and blitz to a thick consistency, adding more liquid as needed. Cool then refrigerate. The purée will thicken up as it cools.

> NOTE: YOU CAN ALSO USE CUMQUATS FOR THIS PURÉE WHEN THEY'RE IN SEASON. THIS MAKES MORE THAN YOU NEED, BUT IT KEEPS REALLY WELL IN THE FRIDGE AND IS GREAT ON TOAST.

SWEET ROSEMARY POPCORN

Heat the vegetable oil in a medium saucepan over a medium–high heat. Add the popping corn, cover with a tight-fitting lid and cook, shaking the pan occasionally as the corn begins to pop, and continuing until all the corn is popped (about 2–3 minutes). Transfer the popped corn to a bowl.

Gently heat the sugar and water in a very small heavy-based saucepan over a low heat until the sugar dissolves. Brush down the side of the pan with a wet pastry brush to stop any crystals from forming. Bring the temperature to 160°C (315°F) then stir through the rosemary and salt, pour this mixture over the popcorn and quickly stir to coat the popcorn.

Spread onto a tray lined with non-stick baking paper to cool and harden then break up and store in an airtight container until needed. This makes more than you need, but it's addictive.

TO SERVE

Sprinkle the sugar over the custard then caramelise with a kitchen blowtorch. Leave aside for the caramel to set.

Place a smear of the orange purée on the edge of the serving plates. Then use a large kitchen spoon to gently crack through the custard and place one serve at a time on the plates.

Top with the chocolate ice cream, scatter with the sweet rosemary popcorn and serve right away.

BT'S TEQUILA CAKE Serves 12

The first time BT ever came to Bodega, he came with his wife and sat right in front of Ben. We were thinking, 'Who is this guy? He looks like a roadie. He looks amazing.' The two of them were completely wild and just having the time of their lives. He paid with his credit card and Ben ran over to check his name. We looked him up and it turned out he was from Love Police, the guys who bring in The Black Keys and a bunch of other bands we love. And then he just started coming in all the time. From then on, he'd send bands our way when they were in town, or sling us free tickets to stuff. We just became really good friends with him. He even lent Elvis an original Nudie suit for his wedding. Anyway, whenever he'd come in he'd always bring a bottle of Hussong's tequila. The year we opened Porteño, BT came in for his birthday and Elvis made a tequila cake, shaped like the bottle, with each layer flavoured with a different tequila. We use darker barrel-aged tequilas on the bottom layers of this cake. Reposado is kind of smoky and goes so well with the chocolate coffee flavours, but you can also just use one type of tequila throughout. You can put as much or as little booze into this cake as you like — this is a rough guide. It's definitely an adults-only cake. It takes a couple of days to make, but it's well worth it. This cake is a nod to BT — he makes our life legendary.

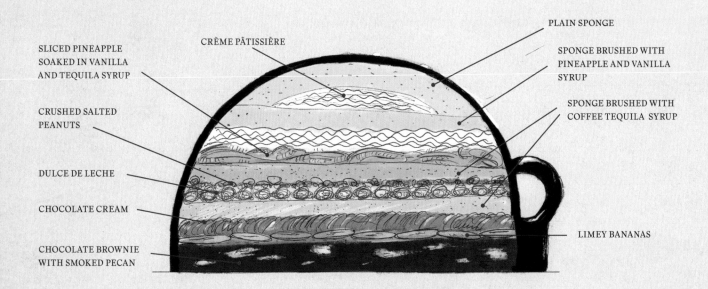

SLICED PINEAPPLE
SOAKED IN VANILLA
AND TEQUILA SYRUP

CRÈME PÂTISSIÈRE

PLAIN SPONGE

SPONGE BRUSHED WITH
PINEAPPLE AND VANILLA
SYRUP

CRUSHED SALTED
PEANUTS

SPONGE BRUSHED WITH
COFFEE TEQUILA SYRUP

DULCE DE LECHE

CHOCOLATE CREAM

LIMEY BANANAS

CHOCOLATE BROWNIE
WITH SMOKED PECAN

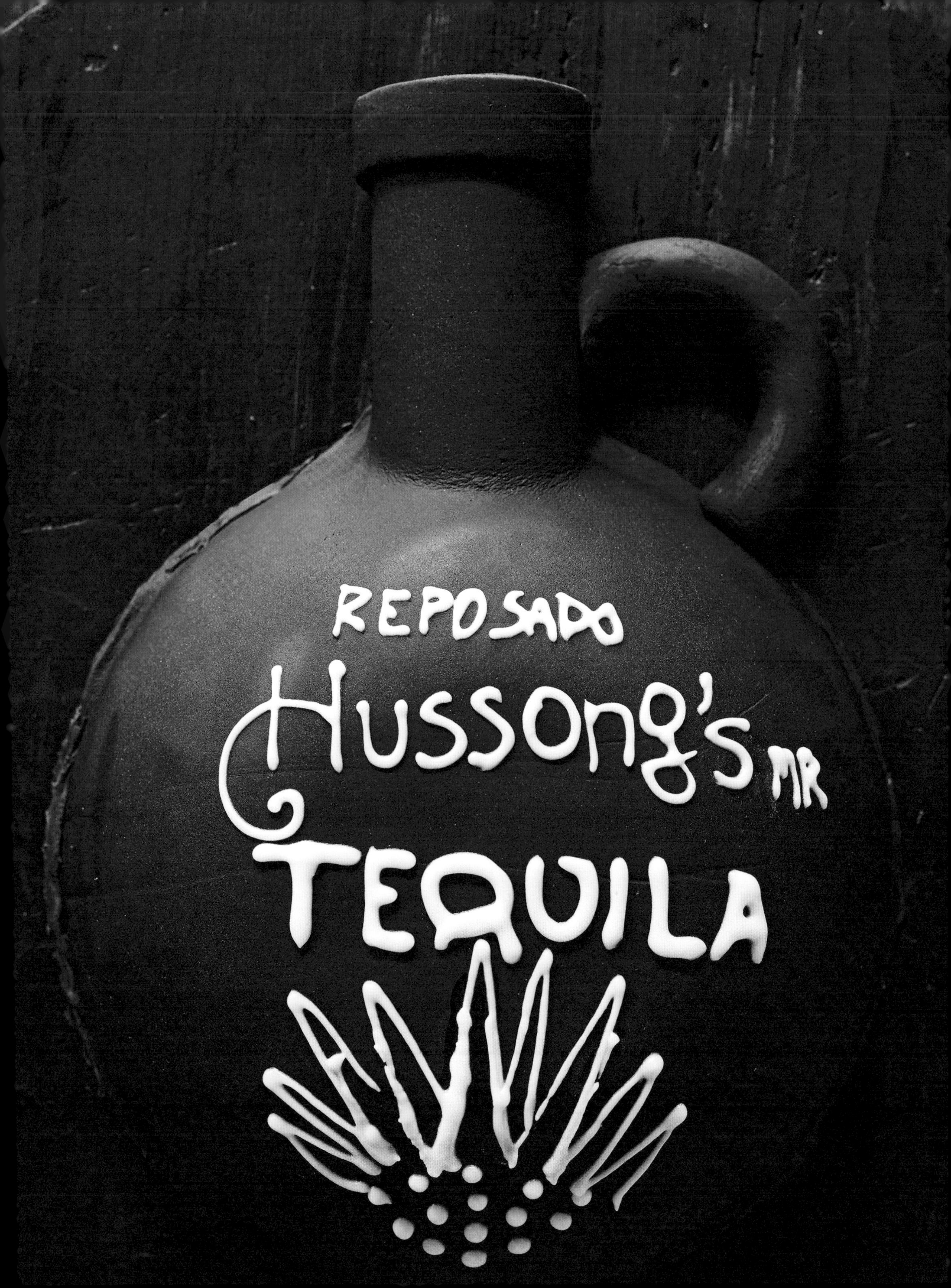
REPOSADO
Hussong's MR
TEQUILA

SPONGE

400 g (14 oz) whole cracked eggs (about 8 eggs)
240 g (8⅝ oz) caster (superfine) sugar
200 g (7 oz) plain (all-purpose) flour, sifted
40 g (1½ oz) almond meal

CHOCOLATE & SMOKED PECAN BROWNIE

135 g (4¾ oz) unsalted butter
135 g (4¾ oz) dark chocolate (64% cocoa solids),
    chopped
125 g (4½ oz) brown sugar
2 eggs, lightly beaten
55 g (1⅞ oz) almond meal
1½ tablespoons unsweetened cocoa powder, sifted
55 g (1⅞ oz) roughly chopped smoked pecans
    (see smoking chart pg 139)

CHOCOLATE CREAM

125 ml (4 fl oz) milk
125 ml (4 fl oz) cream (35% fat)
½ a vanilla bean, split and seeds scraped
45 g (1⅝ oz) caster (superfine) sugar
50 g (1¾ oz) liquid glucose (see Glossary)
50 g (1¾ oz) egg yolks
15 ml (½ fl oz) tequila
100 g (3½ oz) dark chocolate (64% cocoa solids),
    roughly chopped
a pinch of fine sea salt

CRÈME PÂTISSIÈRE

300 ml (10½ fl oz) milk
1 vanilla bean, split and seeds scraped
100 g (3½ oz) caster (superfine) sugar
80 g (2¾ oz) egg yolks (about 4 yolks)
20 g (¾ oz) plain (all-purpose) flour
20 g (¾ oz) cornflour (cornstarch)
20 ml (½ fl oz) tequila

PINEAPPLE & VANILLA TEQUILA SYRUP

1 × 400 g (14 oz) tin of pineapple rings, in juice
1 vanilla bean, split and seeds scraped
30 ml (1 fl oz) tequila

TEQUILA & COFFEE SYRUP

30 g (1 oz) caster (superfine) sugar
30 ml (1 fl oz) boiling water
50 ml (1½ fl oz) espresso
50 ml (1½ fl oz) tequila

LIMEY BANANAS

1–1½ large bananas
juice of 1 lime

ASSEMBLING THE CAKE

150 g (5½ oz) salted peanuts (see pgs 43–45)
250 g (9 oz) dulce de leche

DECORATING & SERVING THE CAKE

350 g royal icing mixture (see note)
1–2 tablespoons water
600 g (1 lb 5 oz) black fondant icing
    (see note)
icing (confectioners') sugar, for dusting

NOTE: FONDANT ICING AND ROYAL ICING
MIXTURE ARE BOTH AVAILABLE FROM
SPECIALIST CAKE SUPPLY STORES,
OR ONLINE.

SPONGE

Preheat the oven to 170°C (325°F/Gas 3). Whisk the eggs and sugar using an electric mixer for about 5 minutes, or until very fluffy. Transfer the mix into a large bowl and carefully fold in the sifted flour then the almond meal using a rubber spatula.

Divide the mixture between two 22 cm (8½ inch) greased, floured and lined round cake tins and bake for 30 minutes, or until a skewer inserted in the centre comes out clean.

Remove from the oven, leave to cool then turn out onto wire racks and set aside to cool to room temperature. Once cool, refrigerate until needed.

CHOCOLATE & SMOKED PECAN BROWNIE

Preheat the oven to 190°C (375°F/Gas 5).

Grease and line a 23 cm (9 inch) round cake tin. Put the butter and chocolate in a heatproof bowl over a saucepan of simmering water. Make sure the bottom of the bowl isn't touching the water. Stir occasionally until melted and smooth then remove from the heat and leave to cool slightly.

Add the sugar to the mixture and then gradually whisk in the beaten eggs before adding the almond meal and cocoa powder. Whisk until just combined. Fold through the chopped pecans then pour the batter into the cake tin and cook in the oven for 15 minutes, or until a skewer inserted in the centre comes out clean.

Leave to cool in the tin, then turn out onto a wire rack to cool completely. Set aside until needed.

CHOCOLATE CREAM

Put the milk, cream and split vanilla bean and seeds in a small saucepan and bring to the boil over a medium heat. Remove from the heat and discard the vanilla bean.

Cream the sugar, glucose and egg yolks together in a bowl until light and fluffy, then pour the hot milk mixture slowly over the sugar mixture, whisking constantly to combine. Return the mixture to the saucepan over a low heat and stir continuously until it reaches 85°C (185°F) but be careful not to split it.

Stir in the tequila.

Put the chocolate in a bowl with a pinch of salt, pour over the hot custard and leave for a minute to melt. Use a whisk to gently and slowly work the mixture from the inside out until the chocolate has all melted and it's nice and smooth.

Leave it in the bowl to cool and whisk every 10 minutes to knock some air into it. Do this until completely cooled down then leave in the fridge to set until you're ready to assemble the cake.

CRÈME PÂTISSIÈRE

Heat the milk and the split vanilla bean and seeds in a small saucepan over a medium heat until hot.

In a large bowl, whisk the sugar, egg yolks, flour and cornflour together really well.

Remove and discard the vanilla bean from the saucepan, then gradually pour the hot milk into the sugar mixture, whisking constantly.

Strain the mixture back into a clean small saucepan and cook over a medium heat, stirring constantly so it doesn't catch or burn. At first, it may appear to be slightly lumpy, but keep stirring for about 5 minutes. Stir in the tequila.

Spoon the mixture into a container and place plastic wrap directly on the surface so it doesn't form a skin. Refrigerate until needed.

PINEAPPLE & VANILLA TEQUILA SYRUP

Pour the juices from the pineapple tin into a bowl and add the vanilla bean and seeds, and the tequila.

Slice the pineapple rings into thin half-moon shapes and place them back in the juice to infuse until needed.

TEQUILA & COFFEE SYRUP

Place the sugar in a heatproof jug and pour over the boiling water, stirring until the sugar is dissolved completely. Add the espresso and tequila and set aside to cool to room temperature.

LIMEY BANANAS

Slice the bananas and put them into a small bowl. Drizzle over the lime juice then place in the fridge until needed.

ASSEMBLING THE CAKE

Get a large round bowl approximately 25 cm (10 inches) wide at the top and 11 cm (4¼ inches) wide at the bottom. It also needs to be 11 cm (4¼ inches) deep. Line it with plastic wrap, allowing it to hang over the sides (this will help you ease out the cake after it sets). Have all of your prepared elements to hand.

Trim the tops from the sponges to level them off, if necessary. Carefully slice each sponge in half so you end up with four rounds approximately 1.5 cm (⅝ inch) thick. Roughly smash the salted peanuts using a mortar and pestle and put aside.

You'll need to trim the sponges to fit the bowl as you go, to make sure they fit snugly. Start with a small circle of the plain sponge and follow that with a layer of crème pat.

Cut out a slightly bigger circle of sponge, brush it generously with the pineapple and vanilla tequila syrup and place on top of the crème pat, brushed side up.

Follow the diagram on page 182 and continue to layer up the ingredients evenly, brushing sponges with syrups where required, and finishing with the final layer of chocolate brownie.

Once finished, fold any overhanging plastic wrap back over the bowl and place it in the fridge. Leave in the fridge overnight to help the cake settle and become compacted.

DECORATING & SERVING THE CAKE

Place the royal icing mixture in a bowl and gradually add a tablespoon of the water, stirring to combine until you have a smooth, pipeable icing that holds its shape. Gradually add more water if needed. Spoon this mixture into a piping (icing) bag with a 5 mm (¼ inch) nozzle. Set aside.

Roll out the fondant icing to a 38 cm (15 inch) round.

Take the cake out of the fridge and unwrap the bowl. Place a large serving plate over the bowl and carefully turn the cake out onto the plate. Remove the bowl and discard any plastic wrap then cover the cake completely with the black fondant. Trim the edges so it looks neat and use these offcuts to shape a neck and handle for the bottle. Pipe the white icing onto the cake, to make it look like a Hussong's Tequila bottle (see page 183) and that's it. Job done.

Alex Atala's
RECIPE FOR A GOOD TIME

TRANSPORT – **Triumph Bonneville**
SOUNDTRACK – **Gene Vincent/ Buddy Holly**
GEOTAG – **Sydney**
WELCOME LADY – **Astonishing blonde girl just in-between
Eva (Evita) Perón and a Vargas girl (Sarah Doyle)**

Mix everything and cook over low heat with a cold beer.
Add two great and cool chefs, Elvis and Ben.
Serve this with lamb on the cross prepared by Elvis's dad.
Enjoy until the end.

God made it. Devil put it all together!

PARILLA

COOKING WITH FIRE

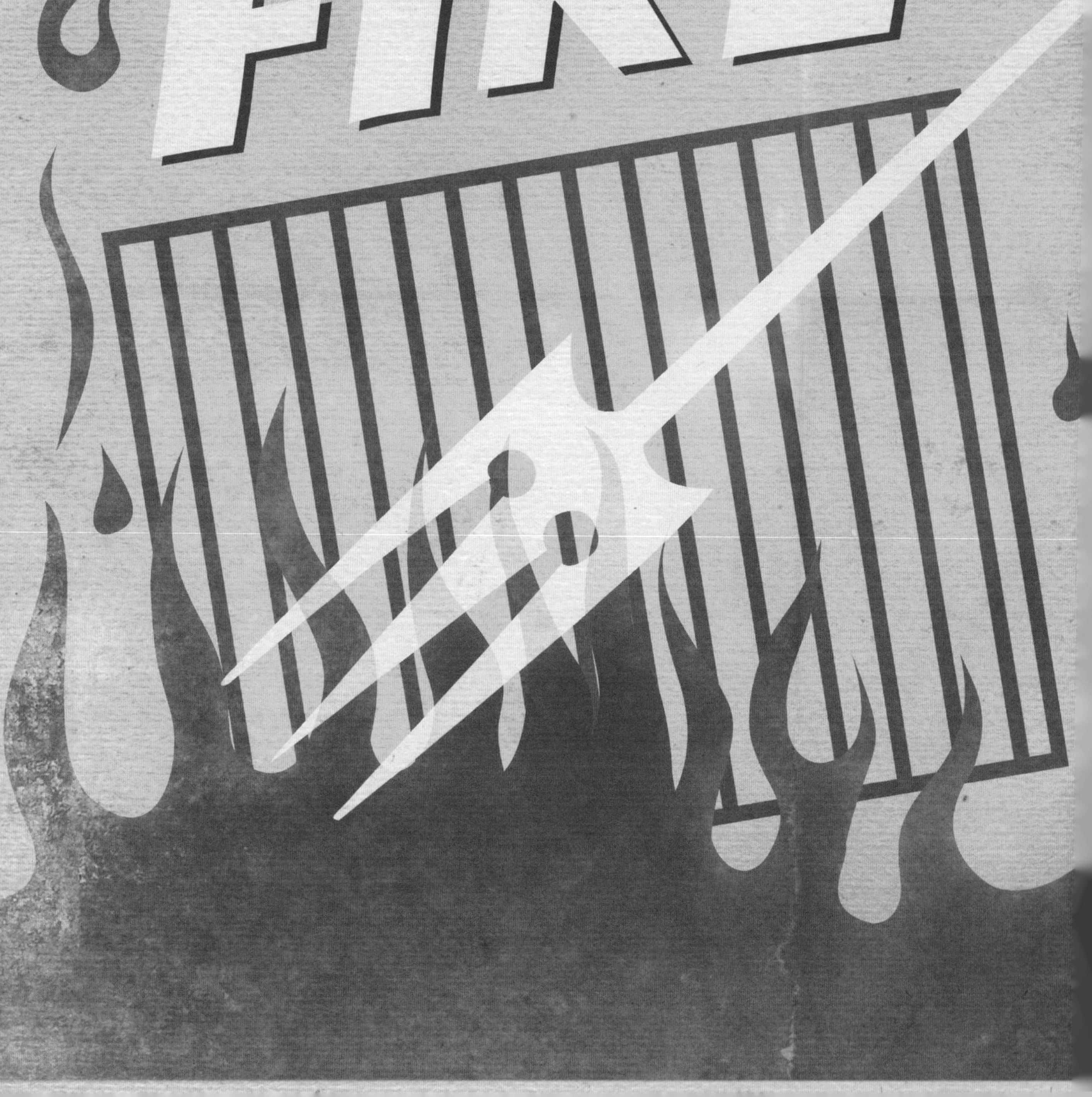

ASADO

Barbecuing over an open fire is the greatest job you can have as a cook, and in Argentina, where Elvis and his family come from, it's what weekend cooking is all about. They'll whip up a fire at any event and it's not about showing off with the latest hi-tech equipment or having a big shiny barbecue, it's about simplicity. Building a proper fire, getting to know how it behaves and learning how to control it are the most important things. That's what this chapter is all about.

Elvis's dad, Adan, is our secret weapon. He's been cooking this way since he was old enough to light a match, and to this day he's still trying new things and perfecting his technique. He makes it all look so easy, carrying pigs on the cross like it's nothing and building perfect fires day-in and day-out at Porteño.

Even for experienced chefs, cooking with fire is like starting from the beginning. It's intuitive, physical and you've got to pay attention. Whenever we think we've nailed something, the old man will come along and show us something new. We love it, and we love the simplicity of meat, salt and fire.

You won't find any formal recipes in this chapter because we don't really have any. This style of cooking is all about trial and error, but anyone can do it and, like anything, you'll get better at it the more you do it. We don't use any marinades or mask the flavour of the meat in any way. We keep things simple and let the produce speak for itself. The only other ingredients are time and patience. That, and enough beer to help you pass the time and stay patient.

As Adan likes to say, 'If the fire's right, the food will taste good.'

"BUILDING A FIRE,
GETTING YOUR
BEAST ON
AND DRINKING
SOME BEERS."

CHOOSING THE WOOD

It's taken two and a half years of constant experimenting and tweaking to get our barbecuing right. At one point we were getting deliveries of wood that were burning black really quickly, but not giving off any heat. We were told by one of our suppliers that when a tree has been struck by lightning, the wood won't burn properly. And if there are termites or holes in the wood, there'll be too much oxygen and you'll get sparks flying off your fire. One delivery had a really exciting bonus: a family of scorpions. We caught one, put it in a glass and poured a shot of Jack Daniel's over it to preserve it.

Today, we burn about a tonne of wood a week, which we get from Blackheath in the Blue Mountains — about a two-hour drive from the restaurant. We use ironbark because it's really dense and burns long and hot. It's also aromatic, but not strong like fruitwood, which is perfect if you're cooking with it all day, every day. If you reckon you need that extra flavour you can always chuck in random pieces of fruity wood like grapevine, peach or whatever you've got as you're cooking. But for us, ironbark is the workhorse.

It's important to have well-cured wood. By that we mean wood that's been left to dry out for at least a few months (if not a year or more) after it's been cut. It really does affect the way the fire burns and the way the meat cooks. If the wood's too wet, the animals are actually steaming instead of roasting.

Elvis's old man has a lot of tricks up his sleeve with this stuff. He'll never tell you them, though, you just have to catch him in action.

BUILDING THE FIRE

We know Elvis's dad likes to heat up the logs around the edges of the pit before putting them on the fire itself: put cold timber on the blaze, he reckons, and you'll kill it. And that's what it's all about: maintaining the height and heat of the fire so it's as even as possible the whole time you're cooking. That's why you've got to stand next to it the entire time.

Waxed fruit boxes is another trick we have up our sleeve. You roll a long strip of the waxed cardboard into a tube about as thick as your arm and a foot long, tie it with string and presto! You've got a chimney for your fire that lets in plenty of oxygen. And, because it's wax, it burns slowly and acts as a built-in firelighter. To make the fire, you start with a circle of charcoal or small bits of wood to hold up the chimney. Then you make a bit of a teepee with more pieces of wax cardboard, and eventually build your way up with larger pieces of wood. Elvis's dad doesn't mind throwing on a splash of metho or really good quality olive oil either (if he thinks no one's looking).

It can be hard to keep that teepee shape, but it's really important you do. At any time it can collapse, then you've got the problem of the fire spreading out, causing everything to heat unevenly. You always want the fire and heat going straight up. Don't put heavy logs all the way around; lean two heavy logs over the fire on one axis, but then have smaller ones across the other axis so you're not suffocating it. Stop the collapse by finding the gaps in the fire as the wood burns away and replacing each piece as it happens. You also don't want the entire circumference of the fire to exceed three feet.

As you can see from these pictures, you can build a great fire anywhere — even a warehouse. Just make sure you stay near it, watching and controlling it, the whole time. If you're going to do this in your backyard, build it well away from any buildings or sheds and make sure you know which way the wind's coming from so you can protect your fire, or make sure to have a back-up plan. It's good to have a few big pieces of corrugated iron on hand just to shield the fire. Wind is the enemy of a good fire. The slightest gust will make your fire weak and uneven — we have that problem at Porteño if the doors are open.

"BARBECUING IS THE
GREATEST JOB YOU CAN
HAVE AS A COOK."

WHOLE BEAST ON THE CROSS

We use different barbecuing techniques at the restaurant and we do a lot of cooking over coals, but we're probably best known for our whole pigs and lambs cooked on the cross over an open fire. This is called *a la cruz*, and it's a method of cooking that's been used for hundreds of years in the wilds of Argentina. It's particularly common in Patagonia and it's thought the shepherds there learned the tradition from the Spanish, who in turn borrowed it from the Arab world. The animal is butterflied over a metal or wooden crucifix that has two crosspieces for trussing both sets of legs. Most of the cooking is done with the inside of the carcass facing the flames, so that the bones protect the meat from the most intense heat and stop it drying out; while conducting the heat evenly through the muscles. Then the animal is usually turned over at the end to finish the other side and crisp up the skin.

Lambs weigh in at around 15 kilos and our pigs weigh about ten, so they're good for a party. The first thing — and this is important — is to take your animal out of the cool room or fridge well ahead of when you're going to start cooking it so that it comes up to temperature. We're talking a good few hours here, depending on the weather. If the meat's too cold it'll take longer to start cooking. If you're doing a whole lamb or pig, you want to flatten it out so you can get it flush on your cross (like the pictures here). You can do this by either cutting from the pelvis and gently cracking the rib bones (you don't want any of the meat exposed), then dislocating the legs. Or, if you're careful and don't mind stamping on your lunch, you can put your animal between two garbage bags and then stand on it till it cries mercy and splays open. Once it's flat, oil and salt the inside of the carcass.

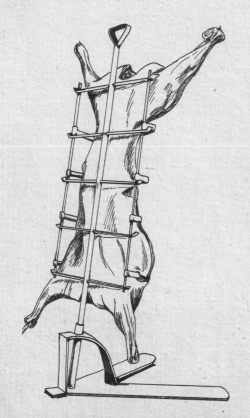

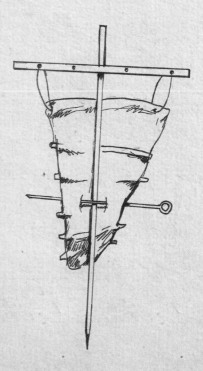

You don't want to put your lamb or pig on if the fire's raging or it'll cook too quickly on the outside. It all needs to heat up gradually. Whatever animal you choose to use, you'll want to cook it bone side first — primarily to protect the meat and stop it from drying out, but also as the bones heat up, they start cooking the meat from the inside, like little heat rods.

We use a purpose-built metal cross we bought in Argentina for our asado and it has clamps attached, but you can just make one out of wood at home and truss your beast with wire. It doesn't really matter what type of wood you use for the cross because it's never going to be close enough to the heat to catch on fire. When you're ready to start cooking, you hammer the whole thing in the ground two feet away from the fire leaning in at about 15 degrees. When it's time to eat, you lift the entire thing onto a bench and carve it off the cross. It doesn't have to be perfect. In Argentina, they don't slice it all neatly and thinly like we do here at the restaurant, they carve off chunks.

While the meat's cooking, we baste it a few times with a saltwater mixture they call *salmuera* in Argentina. It is a mix of 300 g (10½ oz) salt to 1 litre (35 fl oz) of water. The brine can be made with any aromats you like: peppercorns, bay leaves or whatever's lying around. The salt is the thing. You apply this brine three times during the cooking process: once about 20 minutes after the animal starts to cook, the second time in the middle of the process (about two hours in), and the third time about half an hour before you turn it over to crisp up the skin.

The thing about using brine rather than salt is that when you're seasoning this way you get an even layer. This is especially crucial when cooking a pig. If you just use salt you're going to get pockets where it starts curing the skin and other patches where the heat makes it puff up like crackling in an oven. The brine will give the skin an effect like a glaze, or the top of a crème brûlée. The best way to apply it is with a bucket and a good old Chux (or other clean, disposable kitchen cloth), squeezing the brine over. Elvis's dad reckons the brine also needs to be warm. Applying cold saltwater to your roasting animal will slow down the cooking time.

You'll be able to tell when the animal is ready because fat and juices will start pouring freely from the bottom of the carcass. You don't have to pull or cut anything to test it; you'll only lose moisture that way.

One of the best things about cooking a lamb *a la cruz* is that you get to try each cut side by side and experience all the different textures — they even taste different. The neck will be a blushing pink and a little firmer, while the shoulders will be falling off the bone. The belly is all crisp. In fact, the skin is like crackling, and sometimes we'll send out a lamb dish and people will say, 'No, I didn't order the pig.' You've got two sections of the leg, too. You've got the round bit of the leg, which has three distinct muscle structures on it and, when it's cooked properly, each one turns a different colour: grey, white and pink. All the flavours in the lamb rainbow.

GRILLING OVER CHARCOAL: BEASTS

We're here to tell you that sawing a pig's head in half when you're hungover is absolutely horrible. Now you know the real reason we stopped Sunday lunch service at Porteño: not because we were wrecked running two restaurants and needed a day off a week, but because we couldn't hack the sound of sawing through a pig's skull at six in the morning. All the same, a pig's head is delicious. The reason we split the head in two is purely so we can get it flat. We also cut the noses off. It's a bit depressing, but the end result — where the cheeks puff out rather than stretch back against the head — is much better.

Once you've got the pig butterflied, you can either cook it on the cross, like the lamb, or flatten it out over a big wire rack and cook it over charcoal. You'd be surprised how little charcoal you need to cook a pig. The important thing is to make sure the coals are almost white before you start cooking. With vegetables such as roast eggplant (aubergine) or capsicum (pepper), it doesn't matter if the coals aren't completely ready because they have their skins to protect them, but with a pig, the flavour of uncooked charcoal goes right through into the meat and can give you an upset stomach.

With the grill, you always keep the animals quite high and you work the heat more. Four bricks off the ground holding a wire rack is a good height. It's all about minimal charcoal in a circle, with a little extra in the middle. You hardly ever add heat to the centre, but all the way around instead. You want the heat to circulate and spread and you'll need to replace the charcoal as it burns throughout the day. Make sure you have a small pit to the side where you can keep topping up. There's nothing worse than running out of hot coals.

It's important to have at least one other person to help you flip the pig once it's done on one side. It's best to have an extra wire rack on hand, a little bit like placing a plate over a pan when you're flipping a Spanish omelette or else it's a matter of being really careful. Also, make sure you both turn the same way or you run the risk of a twisted pig. Don't let your dinner die for nothing!

The most important thing of all with all of this type of cooking is maintaining a constant, even heat. The big mistake people make with barbecuing is freaking out that it's not happening quickly enough. They'll keep adding more fire, which is wrong. It's all got to happen slowly — you're really just warming the animal. Just have patience. Patience, and a few cold beers handy.

SMALLER CUTS & OTHER THINGS

A big part of the ritual of an Argentinean barbecue (and one we definitely stick to) involves grilling a variety of meat, cuts and vegetables. We usually get the veg out of the way first while the fire is roaring hot and we're waiting for the coals to cool down. Most of the veggies are done over a medium–hot heat, but we'll lower the grill for things like peppers and chillies, which need to be over a slightly higher heat so their skins blacken and blister. It doesn't matter that you're cooking them first because barbecued veggies are great at room temperature; that way you've got time to peel or marinate them before serving. Another bonus of cooking them first is that the grill doesn't get cross-contaminated with meat, which is important for vegetarians.

Once the coals are quite red, with a film of white ash over them, we start putting on the meat. Bigger cuts like brisket and beef ribs go on first because they take the longest, but we also put the chorizo, morcilla, sweetbreads and intestines (*chinchulines*) on then; not because they take a long time, but because we smash those while we're waiting for the rest to cook.

It's really important to take any meat out of the fridge a few hours before grilling so it can come to room temperature first. While that's happening concentrate on getting an even bed of white-hot charcoal on the go, with a little supply of fresh charcoal nearby so you can top up as you cook. It's very important to keep the heat consistent and even, especially when you're cooking bigger cuts of meat.

We usually place the grill about 30 cm (12 inches) above the charcoal and test if it's ready to cook by holding our hand above the fire. If you can hold it there for about five seconds before it gets hot, you're good to go. It should be evenly hot all over — not just in the middle. It's a good idea to keep extra bricks on hand to raise the grill if the meat is cooking too quickly because it's better to do this than disturb the charcoal.

Things like skirt steak and poultry can go on a little later. When meat is on the bone, we cook about 60% of it on the bone side and then flip it over to finish it off. Basically, you want the heat to penetrate through the top before you flip it.

If you can wait, it's important to let everything rest before you eat it. But if you need to carve a hunk of meat up to tide you over while the other cuts rest, that's OK. No one needs to know.

We're mentioning this again because it's important: the meat must always be at room temperature before it's cooked, so get it out of the fridge well ahead of time.

To guide you, we've given you 'hand over heat' temperatures below. This means the length of time you can hold your hand 45 cm (about 18 inches) above the fire before you feel like it's going to burn. It may not be the most conventional way to test the temperature, but it works for us.

LOW = 20 SECONDS
MEDIUM = 10–15 SECONDS
HIGH = 5 SECONDS

BRISKET & SIDES OF BEEF RIBS
(BASED ON 3–4 KG/6 LB 12 OZ–9 LB)
- Temperature: Low heat, similar to cooking a pig over charcoal.
- Cooking time: About 3–4 hours, turning only once.

Tip: Always cook brisket or fatty cuts of beef fat side down, except when they're on the bone like the beef ribs; in that case, start bone side down to allow the heat to penetrate into the bones and through the meat.

WHOLE CHICKEN
(CHICKEN: 1.5–2 KG/3 LB 5 OZ–4 LB 8 OZ)
- Temperature: Medium.
- Preparation: Put the chicken on a board with the legs facing towards you. Pull one leg away from the body and slice through the skin between the leg and the breast. Use kitchen scissors to cut along the side of the breast, up through the ribs towards the wing. Repeat on the other side, then push the breast up and away from you — making sure the breasts remain joined and intact. Open the thighs out, pop each thigh bone out of its socket and do the same with the wings. Cut away the rib bones. Turn the bird over so it's skin side up and flatten it out a bit. But don't squash the breast meat.

- Cooking time: Lay the bird flat on the grill, skin side up, until the warmth comes through the top of the breast (about 25–30 minutes). Flip it over and cook it, skin side down, for a further 10 minutes to crisp up the skin and finish it off. It should be perfectly moist all over.

SAUSAGES & SWEETBREADS
- Temperature: Low–medium.
- Preparation: Prick the sausages before cooking so the fat drips out and prevents them from bursting.
- Sweetbreads need salt before they go on as well as an occasional squeeze of lemon juice throughout the barbecuing process.
- Cooking time: 40–60 minutes. You can always increase the heat towards the end or lower the grill right at the end of cooking if you want a bit more colour.

STEAKS & RIBS
ENTRAÑA (SKIRT STEAK) (350 G/12 OZ)
- Temperature: Medium-hot, depending on how you like your steaks. For us, medium is perfect.
- Preparation: Season lightly with salt.
- Cooking time: Put straight onto the grill, fatty side down, and cook for about 8 minutes. Flip over and cook for about 4 minutes then remove from the heat and rest for about 5 minutes. Put back on the grill for a quick lick (about a minute each side).

SIRLOIN STEAK (400 G/14 OZ)
- Temperature: Medium-hot.
- Cooking time: 3 minutes on each side, remove from the heat and rest for 5 minutes, then put back on for 1½–2 minutes on each side.

BEEF RIBS
- Temperature: Medium-hot.
- Preparation: Cut into 2 cm (¾ inch) ribs (thin ribs).
- Cooking time: Cook for 3–4 minutes on each side. We eat these almost straight away, right off the grill with our hands. That's the best way.

Dan Auerbach's
RECIPE FOR A GOOD TIME

For me, the good times start with good records. My preference
is always a box of hand-picked 45s dating no later than 1971.
A mixture of classic country, soul, psych, rockabilly, Jamaican
roots music, swamp pop, Cajun belters etc. . . . I'm sure you get
the idea. If you want to hang with the Bodega/Porteño gang then
make sure you have your style right. Tuck your shirt in, put on
your old Navajo collar tips and make sure your boots look right
while being comfortable enough to allow for an all-night dance
party. Dazzle with vintage jewellery and accoutrements plucked
from tiny stores in the middle-of-nowhere towns all across the
Americas. I find the evening slides easiest into good times with
a few banana old fashioneds. From there, it's really just letting it
all hang out with your friends and your family. Love one another,
make sure your partner's drink is always full and get on with it.
Thanks Ben and Elvis and the gang. See you all soon I hope . . .

DQA

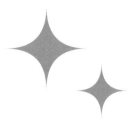

Gardel's

Gardel's bar sits right above Porteño, but it has really become its own little world with its own distinct personality. It's got large windows that run along one side of it so customers can sit up there and watch all the action going on below. We'd never run a bar before this one so that was a little scary. Luckily, we'd spent time in a lot of them and had pretty clear ideas about what we did and didn't like. We named it after the king of tango, Carlos Gardel; he was huge in the '20s and '30s and is still a legend. To us, he represents the glory and glamour of Argentina in those days.

We wanted to stay true to those tango roots when we decorated, and that type of music (not that we ever play it) makes us think of rich reds and golds, so there's lots of that as well as cowhide and leather. The drinks in Gardel's also reflect that era: flamboyant, well dressed and punchy.

One of the greatest things about having our own bar is being able to run upstairs after a shift, hang out with friends, drink the drinks we like and hear music we love. It's beyond good. Throw in a vintage foosball table and we reckon Gardel's has all the elements of a good time you could ever want.

Not many people know this, but this location was one of the first venues in New South Wales to get a late liquor licence when they started giving them out back in the '70s. That's probably why there are so many dodgy stories associated with this place. After the other bars in the area closed, shift workers, gangsters, nurses and politicians would all make their way down Crown Street and pile in. You can imagine the scene. Some of the waiters think this building is haunted; so do we if we're honest. Ben swears a poltergeist keeps nicking the JD.

WHITE ANCHOVIES, SMOKED BONITO PÂTÉ & WATER CRACKERS

SERVES 8

We're both obsessed with anything in a tin — especially fish. We get these beautiful Spanish white anchovies, crack 'em open and serve 'em as is. Then we make water crackers and bonito pâté and serve it all with these amazing green peppers. It's so easy for parties, too. You can either make the individual crackers up for people, or let them make their own. It's really important to have good-quality tinned fish. We've tried so many different white anchovies from different countries over the years, and these boquerones from Spain are incredible.

SMOKED BONITO PÂTÉ

Vacuum-seal the smoked bonito fillets and cook in a temperature-controlled water bath heated to 62°C (144°F) for 10–15 minutes until cooked. Alternatively, you can place the fillets in a ziplock bag and remove all the air by slowly submerging the bag in some water as you seal it. Place the bag in a saucepan of water heated to the same temperature, and use a digital thermometer (and a simmer pad if you have one) to keep the temperature consistent as it cooks.

Remove the skin from the fillets (if still on) then put the flesh in a food processor and blitz to a smooth paste. You can help it along with a small drizzle of olive oil, if need be.

Spoon the paste into a bowl and fold through the mayonnaise and a generous pinch of pepper until incorporated.

Either serve right away, or place in an airtight container and refrigerate for up to 1 week.

TO SERVE

Spread the pâté on water crackers, sprinkle with smoked paprika and serve with some white anchovies and pickled green chillies.

SMOKED BONITO PÂTÉ

2 × 250 g (9 oz) smoked fillets of bonito (see pgs 134–137)
olive oil, if needed
150 g (5½ oz) basic mayo (see pg 274)
freshly ground black pepper

TO SERVE

water crackers (see pg 239)
sweet smoked paprika
4 × 80 g (2¾ oz) tins of marinated white anchovies (boquerones)
pickled green chillies (see pg 278, or buy some Spanish ones)

> THE BEST WAY TO EAT TINNED FISH
> IS LEANING OVER THE SINK.

EMPANADA CODE

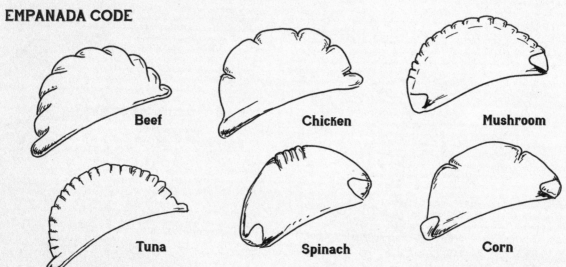

Beef

Chicken

Mushroom

Tuna

Spinach

Corn

EMPANADAS DE CARNE
MAKES 30

MAKE THE FILLING

Heat the extra virgin olive oil in a medium saucepan over a low heat then fry off your onion for 10 minutes, or until softened. Add the spices and cook, stirring for a further 5 minutes then add the meat and cook, stirring occasionally to break up the mince, for 30 minutes, or until the liquid has evaporated and the meat is just starting to fry. Set aside to cool to room temperature. Fold through the eggs and olives and refrigerate to chill.

MAKE THE DOUGH

Melt the ghee in a small saucepan over a low heat.

Put the flour and salt in the bowl of an electric mixer with a dough hook attachment and mix to combine. Mix the melted ghee and water in a jug. Leave the mixer running on a low speed, and gradually add the ghee mixture to the flour until a dough forms. Add another splash or two of water if the dough feels too dry or crumbly. Set aside to rest for 1 hour.

Quarter the dough and roll out to a 2–3 mm ($1/8$ inch) thickness and cut rounds using a lightly floured 15 cm (6 inch) round cutter.

FILL & FRY THE EMPANADAS

Holding a round of dough in one hand, wet the outer edge then place 2 tablespoons of the filling in the centre. Fold the dough over the filling to make a half moon, then press the edges together and fold the lip over itself, pressing and pleating as you go.

Repeat until you've used up all the dough and all the filling. Fill a deep heavy-based saucepan a third full (no more) with oil, and heat the oil to 170°C (325°F). Deep-fry the empanadas in batches for 4–5 minutes, or until golden. Drain on paper towel then serve.

FILLING

60 ml (2 fl oz) extra virgin olive oil
2 brown onions, minced
1 teaspoon sweet paprika
1 teaspoon dried chilli flakes
1 teaspoon ground cumin
fine sea salt and freshly ground
   black pepper
600 g (1 lb 5 oz) minced (ground)
   chuck steak
4 hard-boiled eggs, peeled and chopped
60 g (2¼ oz) pitted black olives,
   chopped

DOUGH

100 g (3½ oz) ghee
500 g (1 lb 2 oz) plain (all-purpose)
   flour
1 teaspoon fine sea salt
250 ml (9 fl oz) warm water

cottonseed oil, for deep-frying

CEVICHE WITH TIGER'S BLOOD

SERVES 8

Blanch the sweet potato in salted boiling water for a few seconds (it should be cooked, but still have a bit of crunch), then cool in ice water and drain.

Place a large saucepan with a lid over a high heat for 3 minutes, or until it is very hot. Have the cleaned mussels and water ready.

Add the mussels and water and quickly put the lid on. The mussels will cook in about a minute (make sure you shake the pan halfway through). Check to see if all the mussels have opened; if not, cook for a further minute until they have.

Strain their cooking liquid into a bowl and put it aside to cool to room temperature. Take the mussels out of their shells and use a small, thin-bladed knife to prise open any that haven't opened to check that they are good. Remove any beards and put the mussels in a clean bowl or plastic container. Cover with their cooled cooking liquid and keep in the fridge.

Shuck the oysters and clams, reserving and straining any of their juices through a fine sieve.

Thinly slice the cuttlefish (you'll need about 8 tablespoons' worth). Dice the kingfish about 1 cm (½ inch) thick (again, you'll need about 8 tablespoons' worth). Thinly slice the scallops.

Strain the mussels through a fine sieve, reserving their liquid, then divide all of the seafood between eight small chilled glasses or shallow champagne saucers.

Blitz the roe, peppers and chilli for the tiger's blood with the combined seafood juices in a blender, then add the extra virgin olive oil and lime juice, to taste. Strain through a fine sieve.

Season the seafood with a pinch of pink salt and drizzle generously with extra virgin olive oil. Add some cooked sweet potato and a few thin slices of red onion.

Whisk the tiger's blood quickly, then pour into the glasses so it comes halfway up the seafood. Garnish with coriander and lime, if using, then serve.

CEVICHE

100 g (3½ oz) sweet potato, peeled
   and cut into 5 mm (¼ inch) dice
16 mussels, scrubbed clean
250 ml (9 fl oz) boiling water
8 small Pacific oysters
8 New Zealand surf clams (vongole)
4 cuttlefish, cleaned and skin removed
200 g (7 oz) sashimi-grade kingfish
   belly, skin off and pinboned
8 scallops
flaked pink salt
extra virgin olive oil
⅛ of a red onion, thinly sliced
a small handful of coriander (cilantro)
   leaves, for garnish
8 thin slices of lime, for garnish
   (optional)

TIGER'S BLOOD

100 g (3½ oz) sea urchin roe
3 piquillo peppers, drained
⅓ of a red bird's eye chilli
500 ml (17 fl oz) reserved juices
   from the seafood and mussels
2 tablespoons extra virgin olive oil
juice of ½ a lime

SALAD OF SMOKED BONITO, PIQUILLO PEPPERS & CELERY

SERVES 8

BONITO

Put the bonito fillets in a non-reactive container. Whisk the brine mixture until the salt and sugar have dissolved, then pour over the fish and cover and refrigerate to lightly brine for 20 minutes. (This is slightly less time than the smoking chart on page 139 says, but that's because we're going to confit the fish as well.)

Remove the fillets from the brine, pat them dry with paper towel then cold smoke them (see pages 134–137) for 15–20 minutes at a medium–high smoke.

Heat the extra virgin olive oil in a small saucepan over a low heat. Add the bonito fillets and poach in the oil, warming them through until they're flaking apart. Remove with a slotted spoon. Once cool enough to handle, peel off and discard the skin, then flake the fish.

TO SERVE

Combine all the vinaigrette ingredients.

Arrange the flaked bonito, sliced celery and leaves, cucumber and piquillo pepper on a plate. Drizzle with the vinaigrette and finish with the sliced spring onion.

BONITO

150 g (5½ oz) bonito fillets, skin on
1 × brine for fish fillets (see pg 139)
300 ml (10½ fl oz) extra virgin olive oil

VINAIGRETTE

40 ml (1¼ fl oz) extra virgin olive oil
40 ml (1¼ fl oz) white vinegar
½ a garlic clove, microplaned
a pinch of fine sea salt

TO SERVE

1 small celery stalk (from the inner section of the bunch), stalk thinly sliced, leaves picked and torn
1 Lebanese (short) cucumber, peeled and thinly sliced
1–1½ piquillo peppers, sliced
1 spring onion (scallion), thinly sliced

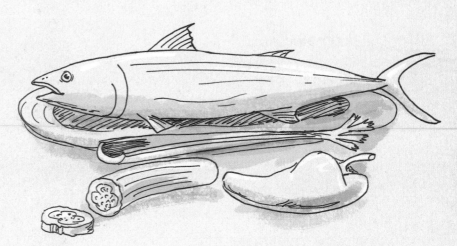

SMOKED OYSTER MAYO WITH MORCILLA

SERVES 8

Shuck the oysters and place them in their half shells on a baking tray lined with slightly scrunched up foil, so they stay flat and their liquid doesn't spill out.

Preheat the oven to 120°C (235°F/Gas ½). Meanwhile, place the oysters in the cold smoker and leave on a high smoke for 15-20 minutes (see pages 138-139).

Take the tray of oysters out of the smoker and place in the oven to bake for 10 minutes, or until just cooked. Chill in the fridge.

Once cooled, remove the oysters from their shells, straining and keeping any liquid. Finely chop the oysters and mix them in with the mayo, shallot and any reserved oyster liquor. Season with salt and a splash of vinegar then store in the fridge.

To serve, preheat the oven to 180°C (350°F/Gas 4). Place the morcilla on a baking tray and heat for 8–10 minutes, just to warm through. You can also heat it on a hot grill, if you like. Break open the skin, scoop the morcilla onto crackers and serve with the smoked oyster mayo.

12 Pacific oysters
charcoal and hickory chips,
    for smoking
250 g (9 oz) basic mayo (see pg 274)
2½ French shallots, minced
fine sea salt
sherry vinegar

TO SERVE
2 × 150 g (5½ oz) morcilla sausages
water crackers (see below)

WATER CRACKERS

MAKES ABOUT 90 CRACKERS

Mix the yeast and water in the bowl of an electric mixer then allow to stand for 5 minutes, until the mixture becomes frothy.

Add the rest of the ingredients and mix, using a dough hook attachment, for about 5–10 minutes, or until the dough reaches a smooth consistency. Take it out, roll into a ball, cover in plastic wrap and refrigerate for 30 minutes.

Preheat the oven to 170°C (325°F/Gas 3). Unwrap the dough, place it on a floured work surface and quarter.

Work with one piece of dough at a time and press to flatten. Using a pasta machine, roll the dough starting with the thickest setting and working your way down. Lightly flour the dough each time you pass it through, until the dough is around 1–2 mm (1/16 inch) thick.

Cut the dough into rounds using a lightly floured 5 cm (2 inch) round cutter then place on baking trays lined with baking paper. Dock each round with a toothpick seven or eight times. You can re-roll the leftover dough if desired to cut more.

Bake the crackers for 12–15 minutes, or until they are an even golden colour.

Cool and store in airtight containers for up to 2 days.

14 g (½ oz) dried yeast
125 ml (4 fl oz) lukewarm water
225 g (8 oz) plain (all-purpose) flour,
    plus extra for dusting
30 g (1 oz) margarine (melted)
17 g (½ oz) fine sea salt
1 tablespoon buttermilk
¼ teaspoon bicarbonate of soda
    (baking soda)

BEER & MISO LAMB RIBS
Serves 8

Preheat a combination oven with a steam function to 100°C (200°F/Gas ½) and 100% steam. Place the ribs on steamer trays and cook for 2 hours. Remove from the oven and leave to cool. You could also do this in a large stovetop steamer for the same amount of time.

With a sharp, heavy knife or a cleaver, slice alongside each rib so you get single, finger-friendly portions. Place these in a non-reactive dish.

Whisk your beer, miso paste and sugar in a large mixing bowl until combined then pour over the lamb ribs and toss to evenly coat. Cover, refrigerate and leave to marinate for 24 hours.

Preheat your oven to 200°C (400°F/Gas 6) and place the marinated lamb ribs on lined baking trays. Bake for 10–15 minutes, or until a golden crust forms over the ribs.

Serve immediately with some radish and cucumber and a little ginger and garlic microplaned over the top.

4 racks of lamb breast (about
   350–400 g/12–14 oz each)
   (see note)

MISO MARINADE
2 × 350 ml (12 fl oz) bottles of
   draught beer
150 g (5½ oz) yellow miso paste
100 g (3½ oz) caster (superfine) sugar

TO SERVE
cold radish, quartered
cold cucumber, quartered
   and cut into pieces
peeled ginger
peeled garlic

> NOTE: IT'S BEST TO USE LAMB RIBS
> WITH AN EVENLY BALANCED FAT-
> TO-MEAT RATIO AS THIS GIVES
> THE BEST RESULT: GELATINOUS
> FATTY GOODNESS, FLAVOURFUL
> MEAT AND CRISP SKIN.

MILK BUN

CHEESEBURGER

We have taken many post-work trips through the McDonald's drive thru, making our own off-the-menu burgers. We've pretty much tried every combo possible, but our favourite is the double cheeseburger on a steamed bun — we've worked out that it's the perfect meat-to-bun ratio. You can't beat perfection, so this recipe is our ode to the cheeseburger. It took us about a year to get it exactly right. The trick to a good bun is heaps of sugar; that's what makes it soft and shiny. These are called milk buns because of the milk and cream in them. You can also bake this dough in a loaf and cut it into squares, which is really good for parties. If you like, you can even fry the edges in clarified butter.

MILK BUNS

Makes 30

Combine the water and yeast in the bowl of an electric mixer and allow to stand for 5 minutes, or until frothy. Heat the milk and cream in a small saucepan over a low–medium heat until lukewarm.

Add the rest of the dry ingredients to the mixer, then add the cream and milk. Attach a dough hook and mix for 5 minutes on medium–high speed. Check the dough; if it's still sticky, mix for 3–4 more minutes on high speed until it comes away from the sides of the bowl.

Oil a large bowl well with the canola spray, place the dough in the bowl, cover with plastic wrap and allow to rest for 1–2 hours, or until doubled in size.

Knock the air out of the dough then weigh it and portion it into 30 even pieces.

Spray a 30 × 33 cm (12 × 13 inch) baking tray about 6 cm (2½ inches) deep with oil.

Hand-roll each piece of dough into a perfect sphere, lightly spraying your hands and the work surface as you go to prevent the dough from sticking. Place the balls into the tray as you go, arranging them five wide and six long. Cover with plastic wrap.

Leave to rise for another 1–2 hours.

Preheat the oven to 220°C (425°F/Gas 7) (have the fan off in your oven, if possible). Bake for 8 minutes, reduce the heat if they look like they are getting too much colour, then bake for a further 8 minutes, or until the buns are light and golden on top. One minute after removing them from the oven, spray the top of the buns heavily with canola oil to give them a nice lustre and prevent them from cracking.

Allow to rest in the tray for 5 minutes, then turn them out onto a wire rack to cool.

2 tablespoons lukewarm water

14 g (½ oz) dried yeast

280 ml (9¾ fl oz) milk

220 ml (7¾ fl oz) cream (35% fat)

720 g (1 lb 9¾ oz) plain (all-purpose) flour

150 g (5½ oz) caster (superfine) sugar

20 g (¾ oz) fine sea salt

canola oil spray

When it comes to a good burger, it's important to have fat, texture and flavour. Every element of a cheeseburger is important; no one ingredient is less important than another, that's what makes it the perfect sandwich. We never work the meat too hard. We mince it three times through a 5 mm (¼ inch) plate, and then we bring the meat together, roll it into the shape we want and wrap it (we Cryovac it, but really tight plastic wrap will also do the trick). After it sets in the freezer, we slice the patties. That way, you're slicing against the grain, so nothing breaks when you bite into it. Cheese-wise, we like a Kraft single. It's Elvis's favourite cheese. You don't want stretch, you want it to turn into a sauce, and soften the burger.

MILK BUNS FILLING NO. 1
THE CHEESEBURGER
MAKES 8 BURGERS

Dice the meat and fit a 5 mm (¼ inch) plate in your mincer. Mince the meat three times, alternating between the cuts as you go to combine them evenly.

Lay a double layer of plastic wrap on the work surface. Avoid working the meat, just gather it together on the plastic wrap and roll tightly, so it compresses to an 8 cm (3¼ inch) diameter roll. Pierce a couple of holes in the plastic wrap to let some of the air out and to help roll it to the correct size. Add more wrap as you go.

Freeze for about 1–2 hours; enough to set the shape but not freeze the meat, as that will make cutting difficult.

Using a very thin, sharp knife, slice the meat into round patties just under 1 cm (½ inch) thick.

Heat two heavy-based frying pans over a medium heat until hot and add the canola oil, then the patties. Sear for about 1 minute on each side, to keep a slightly pink centre, and sprinkle a little salt on each side of the patty while cooking.

Leave the patties to rest for about 1 minute before building the burgers any way you like.

MEAT PATTIES
200 g (7 oz) beef rib meat
200 g (7 oz) beef chuck
200 g (7 oz) skirt steak
40 ml (1¼ fl oz) canola oil
fine sea salt

BUILDING THE BUNS
8 milk buns, halved (see pg 245)
8 cheese slices (processed cheese)
2 dill pickles, sliced (see recipe pg 275)
¼ of a small white onion, finely diced
American mustard
tomato sauce (ketchup)

We're big fans of playing with temperatures and we like eating hot and cold things together. A lot of our dishes play on that. This burger is all about the smoky fattiness of the hot tongue with the cold delicate crab. Some delis we go to sell beef tongue that's already been smoked and cooked, and you can slice and grill that. The other thing you could do is use Spam instead of tongue (seriously, that's what we eat at work). As for the crab, we like to use the best-quality spanner crab meat we can get; something that's already picked. It's expensive, but really worth it. It's funny, we've put the elements together in a different order in the past and we can always taste the difference. So the way we do it now is salsa golf on both buns, grilled tongue, then crab (dressed with a little olive oil and pepper) and then a little bit of chopped lettuce over the top with a little bit of dill and a tiny dice of white onion. And then, when you eat it, you can taste every single element in there. We don't like everything piping hot, we like it at scoffing temperature. Chomp.

MILK BUNS FILLING NO. 2
TONGUE & CRAB
MAKES 8 BURGERS

TONGUE & CRAB
1 × 1.3 kg (3 lb) large fresh ox tongue
blended oil (95% canola + 5% extra
 virgin)
200 g (7 oz) cooked crabmeat
extra virgin olive oil
freshly ground black pepper

BUILDING THE BUNS
salsa golf (see pg 274)
8 milk buns, halved (see pg 245)
¼ of an iceberg lettuce, finely shredded
2 tablespoons finely chopped dill
¼ of a white onion, finely diced

Place the tongue in a large saucepan of salted water over a high heat and bring to the boil. Reduce the heat so it is just ticking away and braise for 2½ hours, or until tender. Remove from the heat and leave in its cooking liquid until cool enough to touch. Keep the liquid.

Peel and discard the skin from the entire tongue then put the tongue in a container, cover with its cooking liquid and refrigerate overnight. This prevents the tongue from drying out and makes it much easier to slice.

The next day, slice across the tongue so you get 5 mm (¼ inch) discs. Lightly oil these with the blended oil then cook on a hot chargrill pan for less than a minute on each side, until you get nice char lines.

Quickly dress the crab with a little extra virgin olive oil and pepper. Put some salsa golf on both halves of each bun, then top with the grilled tongue, crabmeat, lettuce, dill and onion.

We don't marinate our pork shoulder before cooking it. The way we like to do it, which makes the biggest difference to the end result, is put the whole shoulder in a roasting tin that only just holds it, then cover it in marinade, paper and foil. Then we bake it in the oven for 16 hours at 100°C so the marinade cooks into it. When you pull it out the next day, the trick is to let it sit till it's just cool enough to handle. If it's too cold, you can't pull it. Don't be shy to use your mitts when you're pulling pork. A lot of people pull their meat off so it's all flaky, but we like to keep ours in hunks. Another one of our secrets is to take the skin after we've pulled all the meat, chop it up, and then mix it through the pulled meat. It gives it this amazing texture. Most people throw the skin out, but that's the best bit. If you can't get a shoulder, you can also use belly or neck. Belly is awesome because it's got such great fat coverage.

MILK BUNS FILLING NO. 3
PULLED PORK

MAKES 8 BURGERS + EXTRA PORK LEFT OVER

Preheat the oven to 100°C (200°F/Gas ½). Combine all of the marinade ingredients in a blender and purée till smooth.

Place the shoulder in a roasting tin that just fits it and pour over the marinade. Cover with baking paper and a double layer of foil then cook for 16 hours, or until you can lift back the skin and see that the flesh is falling off the bone.

Remove from the oven and allow to cool for 2 hours.

Carefully move the pork to a board. Pull off the skin, chop it finely then put aside. Pull all of the meat off the bone, then mix the chopped skin through the meat.

Spoon the marinade from the roasting tin into a saucepan and reduce over medium heat until thickened. Return the meat and skin to the roasting tin, pour over the hot marinade then mix together thoroughly.

Cram as much pork as you can into each bun then top with a few bits of pickle, mayo and some coriander leaves.

1 whole pork shoulder, bone in (about 4 kg/9 lb) (see note)

MARINADE
80 ml (2½ fl oz) fish sauce
80 ml (2½ fl oz) soy sauce
40 ml (1¼ fl oz) sherry vinegar
25 ml (¾ fl oz) sesame oil
1 tablespoon smoked paprika
250 g (9 oz) molasses
6 garlic cloves
200 g (7 oz) tinned chipotle chillies in adobo sauce
1 × 400 g (14 oz) tin of piquillo peppers, drained
1 brown onion, roughly chopped

BUILDING THE BUNS
30 milk buns, halved (see pg 245)
30 pieces of butter pickles (see pg 279)
basic mayo (see pg 274)
a handful of coriander (cilantro) leaves

NOTE: IF YOU'RE SLOW-COOKING FOR THIS LONG, IT'S NOT WORTH COOKING A SMALLER PIECE OF MEAT. JUST FREEZE THE LEFTOVERS IN BATCHES, DEFROST OVERNIGHT AND USE FOR OTHER MEALS.

SMOKED CHICKEN WINGS

SERVES 8

Take a chicken wing and pull from tip to end to stretch it out. While stretching, slice through the wing tip joint bone, removing the tip. (Save those for the animal sauce on page 271.)

Slice through the connecting bone joint in the centre of the wing. The knife should slide straight through the cartilage and the ball of the bone. You will now have two pieces of wing prepared, so repeat the process with the remaining wings, and evenly stack them in a non-reactive container.

Whisk the brine mixture until the salt and sugar have dissolved. The quality of your ingredients will give variations, but overall your brine should be sweet and salty to taste, but also evenly balanced — make adjustments as needed.

Pour the brine over the wings and refrigerate for 4 hours.

Remove the wings from the fridge and evenly space them on wire racks over trays so none are touching each other then put them in the fridge overnight to allow the brine to dry and become tacky; this will help the smoke to stick to the wings.

Using a cold smoker, smoke the wings for 2 hours at a medium–high smoke, replacing the coals and hickory chips halfway through with fresh ones.

Preheat a combination oven with a steam function to 100°C (200°F/Gas ½). Leave the wings on the racks and place them in the oven to cook at full steam for 20 minutes. Alternatively, you could cook these in a large stovetop steamer for the same amount of time.

Place the potato starch in a large bowl, add a few wings at a time and toss in the starch to coat, flicking in a little water to help the starch stick to the wings. Fill a deep heavy-based saucepan a third full (no more) with oil and heat to 180°C (350°F). Deep-fry the wings in batches for about 4 minutes, or until dark golden brown and crisp. Serve with some Porteño hot sauce.

CHICKEN WINGS
12 extra large chicken wings
  (about 2 kg/4 lb 8 oz)
1 × chicken wing brine (see pg 139)
charcoal and hickory chips, for
  smoking (see pages 138–139)

DEEP-FRYING
300 g (10½ oz) potato starch
cottonseed oil

Porteño hot sauce (see pg 273),
  to serve

MUSSELS, PALM HEARTS & BLACK BEAN DRESSING
SERVES 8

BLACK BEAN DRESSING

Chop the garlic, chilli and black beans as finely as possible and place in a very small saucepan with the oil (the oil should cover the black beans completely).

Place over a very low heat (it is good to use a simmer pad if you have one) and cook so it is just gently ticking over for around 1 hour.

Let the mixture cool down completely, add the sherry vinegar and transfer to a container for storage in the fridge. This will keep in the fridge for up to 1 month.

MUSSELS

Place a large dry saucepan with a lid over a high heat for 3 minutes, or until it is very hot. Have the cleaned mussels, coriander, ginger and water ready. Add them all to the pan once it's up to heat and quickly put the lid on.

The mussels will cook in about a minute (make sure you shake the pan halfway through). Check to see if all the mussels have opened; if not, cook for a further minute until they have.

Strain the cooking liquid into a bowl and put aside to cool to room temperature.

Take the mussels out of their shells and use a small, thin-bladed knife to carefully prise open any that haven't opened to check that they are good. Remove any beards then put the mussels in a clean bowl or plastic container. Cover them with their cooled cooking liquid and refrigerate.

TO SERVE

Spoon the desired amount of mussels into a bowl with a little of their cooking liquid.

Slice the palm hearts into rings and add them to the mussels with a few spoonfuls of the black bean dressing. Mix together, adjust the sharpness with more vinegar if required, then garnish with chives and serve.

MUSSELS

1 kg (2 lb 4 oz) mussels, scrubbed clean

10 coriander (cilantro) stems with roots

a small knob of ginger, sliced

250 ml (9 fl oz) water

3 preserved palm hearts, drained

sherry vinegar, for drizzling

chopped chives, for garnish

BLACK BEAN DRESSING

1 garlic clove

½ a red bird's eye chilli

50 g (1¾ oz) dried salted black beans (see Glossary)

250 ml (9 fl oz) blended oil (95% canola + 5% extra virgin)

75 ml (2¾ fl oz) sherry vinegar

ANDALUSIAN BUCK

INGREDIENTS
1 teaspoon demerara sugar syrup (see below)
30 ml (1 fl oz) gin
30 ml (1 fl oz) Amontillado sherry
1 tablespoon freshly squeezed
    lime juice
ginger beer, to top

Glass: Goblet/highball
Garnish: Lime wedge

DEMERARA SUGAR SYRUP
Combine two parts demerara sugar to one part
hot water, stirring until the sugar is thoroughly
dissolved.

METHOD
Shake all of the ingredients, except the ginger
beer, with ice then strain into a goblet or highball
glass. Fill with ice, top with ginger beer and
garnish with a lime wedge.

> NOTE: THIS IS A RECIPE ADAPTED FROM
> JEFFREY MORGENTHALER OF CLYDE
> COMMON IN THE STATES.

GARDEL'S DARK & STORMY

INGREDIENTS
30 ml (1 fl oz) honey and ginger syrup (see below)
30 ml (1 fl oz) Gosling's dark rum (or any good
    dark rum)
juice of ½ a lime (squeezed using a Mexican elbow
    squeezer. Keep the lime shell.)
soda water, to top

Glass: Rocks
Garnish: Lime shell (from above)

HONEY & GINGER SYRUP
Combine equal parts freshly squeezed ginger juice
and honey in a jar and shake well until the honey
is thoroughly dissolved. This will keep in the
fridge for 1 week.

METHOD
Pour all of the ingredients, except the soda water,
into your rocks glass. Fill with ice and then top with
soda. Stir gently and garnish with the lime shell.

BANANA OLD FASHIONED

This cocktail's a little bit sneaky because it's so smooth. There's no groundbreaking recipe here really, just bananas in Jack Daniel's. The banana softens the JD, and takes away the heat and the burn. It makes it so smooth it's like you're not even drinking whiskey. It almost makes it a little bit syrupy and changes the texture, too. It's also our friend BT's favourite drink. He celebrated his most recent birthday with friends at Bodega so we made up a big batch. That was also the last night The Black Keys guys were in town and we were all just standing around necking it straight out of the bottle. Dan liked it so much that the first thing he did when he got back to Nashville was brew up a few batches of what we also call ape juice. Wow.

BANANA OLD FASHIONED

INGREDIENTS
50 ml (1½ fl oz) banana-infused Jack Daniel's
(see below)
2 teaspoons smoked maple syrup
(see below)

Glass: Stemless wine/old-fashioned
Garnish: None

BANANA-INFUSED JACK
Pour one 750 ml (26 fl oz) bottle of Jack Daniel's
into a large sterilised mason (preserving) jar
(save the JD bottle). Add 1–1½ large, chopped ripe
bananas then seal. Leave for 1–3 days and have a
taste each day to check the development of flavour;
it's ready when the liquid tastes of banana and has
a good 'mouth feel'. Strain through a fine sieve (save
the bananas for the boozy banana cake on page 88
if you like, you'll need two bottles' worth of bananas
for that), and pour the whiskey back into the JD
bottle. Store at room temperature.

SMOKED MAPLE SYRUP
Place 250 ml (9 fl oz) of pure maple syrup in a bowl
and cold smoke (see pages 138–139) for 30 minutes.
Store in a bottle at room temperature.

TO SERVE
Pour your whiskey and smoked maple syrup into
a glass over a large ice cube and stir several times
before serving.

ARGENTIKI

INGREDIENTS
60 ml (2 fl oz) toasted coconut-
infused rum (see below)
1 tablespoon freshly squeezed
lemon juice
2 teaspoons pineapple juice
(freshly juiced or quality store bought)
1 generous scoop of quality store-bought
pineapple sorbet
2 dashes of Angostura bitters

Glass: Fizz/spider
Garnish: 2 pineapple spears and a pineapple wedge
(skin on)

TOASTED COCONUT-INFUSED RUM
Pour one 750 ml (26 fl oz) bottle of good-quality white
rum into a large sterilised mason (preserving) jar
(save the rum bottle). Add 50 g (1¾ oz) of lightly
toasted desiccated coconut, seal and leave to infuse
for 3 days.

Strain through a fine sieve and discard the
coconut. Pour back into your rum bottle and store
at room temperature.

METHOD
Shake all of the ingredients briskly with ice
to emulsify the sorbet then strain into an
ice-filled glass.

EL NIÑO

INGREDIENTS
50 ml (1½ fl oz) Blanco Tequila
1 tablespoon freshly juiced
 cucumber juice
1 tablespoon freshly squeezed lime juice
2 teaspoons agave nectar
1 teaspoon jalapeño sauce

Glass: Martini/cocktail
Garnish: Lime wedge, coriander salt for rim
 (see below)

CORIANDER SALT
Place a bunch of fresh coriander (cilantro) stems
between two dry disposable kitchen cloths (like
Chux) and store in a warm dry place (like on top
of your oven or a coffee machine) overnight, or
until dry and crispy. Once dry, put in a mortar
with 130 g (4¾ oz) of good-quality river salt flakes
and pound to a fine powder with a pestle. Store
in an airtight container.

JALAPEÑO SAUCE
Add one bottle of green Tabasco and the same
amount of water to a blender and blitz with a large
handful of fresh coriander (cilantro) leaves. Fine
strain and it's ready to use. Store in a container in
the fridge for up to 1 month.

METHOD
Wet half the rim of the martini or cocktail glass
using a lime wedge and gently dip it into the
coriander salt to coat evenly.

Add all the ingredients to a shaker with ice. Shake
hard and fast, then fine strain into your salt-rimmed
martini or cocktail glass.

MEZCAL MICHELADA

INGREDIENTS
30 ml (1 fl oz) mezcal (see Glossary)
2 teaspoons–1 tablespoon chipotle hot
 sauce (depending on how spicy
 you like it!)
juice of ½ a lime
lager, to top

Glass: Highball
Garnish: 2 lime wedges, coriander salt for rim
 (see El Niño)

METHOD
Wet the rim of the highball glass using one of the
lime wedges and gently dip it into the coriander
salt to coat evenly.

Add all of the ingredients, except the lager, to
the glass. Fill with ice and then top with a splash
of lager. Gently stir to combine.

Garnish with lime wedges.

PICKLES & SAUCES

We make all of our own pickles and sauces in-house in large batches that we flavour to our specific tastes. As a rule of thumb, if the brine tastes good then the product is going to taste good.

At Porteño, we make something we call 'animal stock', which is an important background flavour and base to lots of our dishes. Because we barbecue whole animals every day, we always have large quantities of bones on hand and we'll cram as many of these as we can into huge stockpots and simmer them overnight to make the animal stock. We ladle that over stacks of sliced meat before serving, use it as a base for soups and other dishes, or reduce it down with smoked chicken bones to make a sticky intense animal sauce, which we use as our house barbecue sauce.

We pickle all types of vegetables and put them with a variety of dishes. We'll even use some of the pickling liquor for finishing off certain salads because it takes on its own characteristics.

After service, when we're drinking, we'll open a few jars of pickles behind the bar and have picklebacks: a shot of booze, a shot of pickling liquor and then a beer. Our mate BT loves them, and he loves the pickle liquor more than anything. It can give you the worst heartburn but he sips on it like it's a fine cognac. We had some strong pickled baby onions once and those picklebacks were intense (plus they gave us the worst breath).

Occasionally we buy in certain pickles. There's a brand out of Brooklyn that does these amazing pickled gherkins with habañeros. After we've used them up we'll save their liquor, add our own fresh veggies — okra, gherkins or whatever is around — then top up the jar with some fresh vinegar and pimp up the flavours. We figure it's taken months to get the pickling liquor to that point, so we may as well keep it. If you've got a jar of pickles at home you can do the same. Give those new veggies a couple of months and they'll be brilliant. Then maybe invite BT round and let him drink the liquor.

ANIMAL STOCK

Makes 3 litres (105 fl oz)

Animal stock is the base for a lot of our dishes. It's basically a stock made from the roasted bones of all the animals we barbecue at the restaurant. We know not everyone's going to have a whole lamb or pig carcass lying around after an all-day barbecue, so you can use the bones from a roast. It's best to make it the same day you've roasted the bones then freeze the stock, but if you don't have enough bones you could also save any cooked bones in the freezer until you have a good amount. We also use this stock as the base for our barbecue sauce. We've scaled down the recipe for a smaller batch, but use as many bones as you can and think of this as a general guideline.

2 brown onions, skins on, quartered

1 leek, halved lengthways

4 spring onions (scallions)

3 kg (6 lb 12 oz) cooked animal
  bones

Chargrill the onions and leek on a barbecue over medium–hot coals. Ensure a nice dark char on the exposed flesh then place in a large stockpot.

Add the leek, spring onions and animal bones then cover with 6 litres (210 fl oz) of water and bring to the boil over a medium heat.

Reduce to a very low heat and simmer for 6 hours, or until reduced by half. The stock should be steaming and just ticking over with tiny bubbles (put the pot half-off the heat if need be). Skim away any impurities or fat from the surface of the stock as it cooks.

Remove from the heat, strain and remove the bones and veg, then leave to cool to room temperature before refrigerating. This is your animal stock. You can either use it up over the next few days in soups, stews or meat dishes (we'll often ladle some hot stock over carved meat before serving), or you can freeze it in small bags to use up as needed.

ANIMAL SAUCE

Makes about 500 ml (17 fl oz)

To turn the animal stock into sauce, preheat the oven to 200°C (400°F/Gas 6) and roughly chop the chicken carcasses.

Put the chicken carcasses into a large roasting tin and cold smoke for 20 minutes (see the smoking chart on page 139).

Transfer the roasting tin of smoked chicken to the oven and roast for 45 minutes, or until golden brown.

Put all the bones into a stockpot and cover with the animal stock. Simmer so just ticking over for 3 hours, then strain to get rid of the bones.

Strain again through muslin (cheesecloth) then put in a clean saucepan and place over a medium heat until the sauce has reduced down to around 500 ml (17 fl oz). Allow to cool, then transfer to a sterilised bottle and refrigerate until needed. It will keep in the fridge for up to 2 weeks.

3 raw chicken carcasses
2 litres (70 fl oz) animal stock
  (see opposite page)

BODEGA BARBECUE SAUCE

Makes about 250 ml (9 fl oz)

250 ml (9 fl oz) animal sauce
  (see pg 271)
4 tablespoons tomato sauce (ketchup)
1 tablespoon worcestershire sauce
1 tablespoon Sriracha chilli sauce
freshly ground black pepper (to taste)
1 tablespoon molasses
1 tablespoon potato starch
1 tablespoon water

Combine all of the ingredients, except the potato starch and water, in a medium saucepan and bring to the boil over a medium heat.

Mix the potato starch and water together in a small bowl until the mixture becomes a thick slurry (the texture of glue).

Whisk that slurry into the boiling sauce then strain and serve warm. Place any leftovers in a bottle or jar and store in the fridge. It will keep for up to 2 weeks.

CHILLI OIL

Makes 375 ml (13 fl oz)

250 ml (9 fl oz) blended oil (95%
  canola + 5% extra virgin)
25 g (1 oz) red bird's eye chillies
125 ml (4 fl oz) extra virgin olive oil

Place the blended oil and chillies in a small deep saucepan over a low heat.

Cook for 1 hour (take care at the start as the chillies can spit) until all of the moisture has cooked out of the chillies. Leave to cool.

Add the extra virgin olive oil then strain into a container and store. This will keep in the fridge for up to 2 months.

PORTEÑO HOT SAUCE

Makes 550 ml (19 fl oz)

Roughly chop the chillies and discard the stalks.

Place all of the ingredients in a large saucepan and bring to the boil over a medium heat. Once boiling, turn down and simmer for 5 minutes.

Remove from the heat, allow to cool a little then put in a blender and mix until smooth.

Place the mixture in a container then cover and leave in the fridge for 2 weeks so the flavours can develop.

Pass through a fine sieve, taste and adjust the seasoning to your liking (adding more salt or sugar if needed).

Put in a bottle or jar and store in the fridge. It will keep for up to 3 months.

500 g (1 lb 2 oz) long red chillies
500 ml (17 fl oz) white vinegar
2 tablespoons fine sea salt
2 tablespoons caster (superfine) sugar

CHIMICHURRI

Makes 400 ml (14 fl oz)

Put all of the ingredients, except the salt and pepper, in a food processor and pulse until a coarse paste forms.

Season to taste then refrigerate until required. This will keep for a couple of weeks. The colour will change, but that's OK. It will still taste really good.

250 ml (9 fl oz) blended oil (95% canola + 5% extra virgin)
100 ml (3½ fl oz) white wine vinegar
55 g (2 oz) flat-leaf (Italian) parsley leaves
3 garlic cloves, coarsely chopped
3 tablespoons dried oregano
1 tablespoon dried chilli flakes (or more or less, according to your taste)
fine sea salt and freshly ground black pepper

BASIC MAYO

Makes 400 g (14 oz)

TIP: TO TURN THIS MAYO INTO AIOLI, MICROPLANE 2 GARLIC CLOVES INTO THE FINISHED MAYO AND STIR THROUGH.

2 egg yolks
1½ teaspoons dijon mustard
1½ teaspoons sherry vinegar
1½ teaspoons lemon juice
½ teaspoon flaked salt
400 ml (14 fl oz) blended oil
   (95% canola oil + 5% extra virgin)

Blitz all the ingredients (except the oil) in a jug using a hand-held stick blender while slowly adding the oil in a thin stream until all of it is incorporated (you could also whisk this by hand in a bowl while you add the oil).

If the mayo looks too thick, add a tablespoon of warm water to thin it out slightly and make it a little paler in colour. But if you're making this for the smoked oyster mayo (page 239) or the morcilla and scallops (page 12), don't add any water.

CHIPOTLE MAYO

Makes 500 ml (17 fl oz)

2 egg yolks
2 teaspoons American mustard
50 g (1¾ oz) tinned chipotle peppers
   in adobo sauce
1½ tablespoons sherry vinegar
400 ml (14 fl oz) blended oil
   (95% canola + 5% extra virgin)

Blitz the egg yolks, mustard, peppers and vinegar to a paste in a food processor.

Leave the food processor running and gradually add the oil until it's all incorporated.

Add a splash of hot water if the mayo is a little too thick then pour into an airtight container and refrigerate until needed. Use up within the week.

SALSA GOLF

Makes about 250 ml (9 fl oz)

1 egg yolk
1 tablespoon American mustard
3 tablespoons tomato sauce
   (ketchup)
1 tablespoon worcestershire sauce
1 tablespoon fish sauce (optional)
1 tablespoon Sriracha sauce
250 ml (9 fl oz) blended oil
   (95% canola + 5% extra virgin)

Whisk the egg yolk, mustard and sauces together in a bowl.

Continue to whisk as you slowly add the oil, until thick and all incorporated.

Pour into an airtight container and refrigerate until needed. Use up within the week.

DILL PICKLES

Makes one 2 litre (70 fl oz) jar

Remove any leaves or nodules from the ends of the baby cucumbers, then layer them up in a sterilised pickling jar with the dill and sliced onion.

Place your vinegar, water, salt, sugar and mustard seeds in a large saucepan and whisk to dissolve the salt and sugar. Bring the mix to the boil over a medium heat, then set aside and allow to cool. Pour the cooled pickling liquor into the jar of cucumbers so they're totally submerged, then seal, refrigerate and leave for at least 2 weeks before using.

These will keep for a couple of months in the fridge. Once opened, top up with fresh vinegar as needed, to keep everything covered.

1 kg (2 lb 4 oz) baby Lebanese (short) cucumbers

2 bunches of dill, picked

1 brown onion, thinly sliced

330 ml (11¼ fl oz) white wine vinegar

630 ml (21½ fl oz) water

65 g (2⅓ oz) fine sea salt

110 g (3¾ oz) caster (superfine) sugar

1½ tablespoons yellow mustard seeds

PICKLED CELERY

Makes one 2 litre (70 fl oz) jar

Trim the leaves and branches from the celery stalks then wash thoroughly.

Cut the celery into long lengths, checking against the jar to make sure they will fit inside. Place in a glass or ceramic tray, sprinkle with 1½ teaspoons of the salt then toss to evenly coat. Leave them in the tray for 1 hour; the salt will leach some of the moisture from the celery allowing the pickling liquor to replace it later.

Slice the chillies thinly and julienne the ginger. Whisk the remaining salt with the sugar and vinegar in a large bowl until dissolved, then taste and check the balance of sweet, salt and acid. Adjust your salt and sugar levels by adding some of the water.

Rinse the celery under cold water to get rid of the excess salt then put in the sterilised jar and cover with the pickling liquor so they're totally submerged. Add the ginger and chilli then seal and refrigerate for at least 2 days before using.

These will keep for a couple of months in the refrigerator. Once opened, top up with fresh vinegar as needed, to keep everything covered.

650 g (1 lb 7 oz) celery

90 g (3¼ oz) fine sea salt

1½ red bird's eye chillies

½ a knob of ginger

110 g (3¾ oz) caster (superfine) sugar

600 ml (21 fl oz) white vinegar

125 ml (4 fl oz) water

M.Sc

BBQ.Sce

G.PIKLE

CHILLI.MAPLE

PICKLED GREEN CHILLIES

Makes one 2 litre (70 fl oz) jar

1 kg (2 lb 4 oz) long green chillies

2 tablespoons fine sea salt

2 tablespoons caster (superfine) sugar

2 litres (70 fl oz) white vinegar, plus extra to top up

Neatly arrange the chillies so they stand up in the pickling jar. Pack them tightly to the top of the jar. Add the salt and sugar then fill the jar up with vinegar so everything is totally submerged.

Seal tightly, then give the jar a good shake to mix the salt and sugar through evenly. Store in the fridge for 1 week. After a week, the chillies will have started to absorb the pickling liquor and the jar will need to be topped up with fresh vinegar and shaken again.

Store in a cool place for a month before using. The chillies will lose their shine and turn a dull green, but they will taste amazing.

Once opened, top up with fresh vinegar, as needed.

PICKLED GREEN TOMATOES

Makes about 500 g (1 lb 2 oz)

550 g (1 lb 4 oz) green tomatoes

65 g (2⅓ oz) fine sea salt

1 litre (35 fl oz) white vinegar

1 red bird's eye chilli, halved lengthways

4 cardamom pods

1 star anise

1 teaspoon yellow mustard seeds

55 g (2 oz) caster (superfine) sugar

Quarter the tomatoes (or leave them whole, if you prefer). Place them in the jar you're going to pickle them in, then liberally salt them and leave in the fridge overnight.

The next day, bring the vinegar, chilli, spices and sugar to the boil in a small heavy-based saucepan. Cool to room temperature then pour all over the salted tomatoes until completely submerged.

Leave covered in the fridge for at least 2 weeks before using. These will keep in the fridge for up to 2 months. Once opened, top up with fresh vinegar as needed, to keep everything covered.

BUTTER PICKLES

Makes one 2 litre (70 fl oz) jar

Remove the ends from the cucumbers then slice into 8 mm (⅜ inch) rounds and put in a non-reactive container. Sprinkle the salt evenly over the cucumber then allow to sit for 2 hours.

Meanwhile, place the vinegar in a medium saucepan and add the spices. Bring to the boil over a medium heat then remove from the heat and allow to cool.

Once the vinegar has cooled to room temperature, add the sugar and whisk until dissolved to create the pickling liquor.

Transfer the salted cucumbers (and any of their salty liquid) to a large jar. Top up with the pickling liquor so the cucumbers are completely submerged, and store in the fridge for a minimum of 2 weeks before using. These will keep in the fridge for up to 2 months. Once opened, top up with fresh vinegar as needed.

1 kg (2 lb 4 oz) Lebanese (short) cucumbers
2 tablespoons fine sea salt
1 litre (35 fl oz) white vinegar
1 teaspoon ground turmeric
2 teaspoons yellow mustard seeds
¼ teaspoon dried chilli flakes
55 g (2 oz) caster (superfine) sugar

PRESERVED LEMONS

Makes two 2 litre (70 fl oz) jars

Nearly quarter the lemons, but don't cut all the way through them — the base should hold the lemon together.

Break up the cinnamon sticks a bit, then mix with the salt and spices. Push some of that spiced salt inside the lemons.

Pack the lemons tightly into the jars, filling any gaps with the salt mixture and bay leaves as you go. Seal and keep in the fridge or a cool place for a couple of months, or until the peel is translucent and the lemon is soft and cured through. Rinse before using and remove any pith. These will keep for a few months.

12 lemons
2 cinnamon sticks
2.5 kg (5 lb 8 oz) baker's salt
10 cardamom pods
10 star anise
12 fresh bay leaves

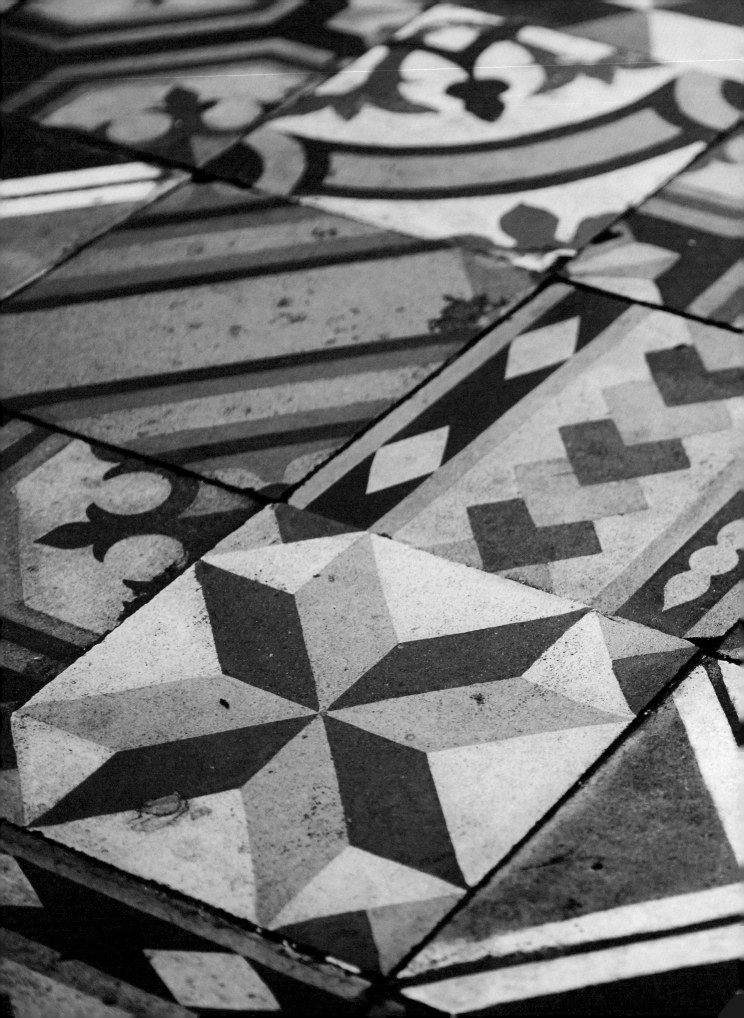

GLOSSARY

Bacalao (salt cod) is the Spanish word for dried and salted cod (bacalhau in Portuguese and baccala in Italian). It is usually soaked before cooking to help rehydrate and soften the fish, and also to remove the excess salt. The centre cut (lomo) is considered the best as the outer cuts can be quite chewy. You should be able to find it at Spanish, Italian and Portuguese delicatessens, online stockists and most fish markets.

Brik (brick) pastry is a North African pastry used for sweet and savoury dishes. It is often deep-fried to create a golden, crispy texture similar to that of phyllo (filo) pastry. It comes in sheets roughly 20–30 cm (8–12 inches) in size and is widely available from the refrigerated section of specialty food stores.

Dextrose (also known as glucose) is not as sweet as standard sugar and caramelises at a lower temperature so it keeps things nice and soft as they start to set. It's widely available from supermarkets and health food stores.

Dried black turtle beans (not to be confused with the dried salted black beans below) are a staple of South American cooking. They are available from specialty food stores and online stockists, and need to be soaked for several hours then drained before cooking.

Dried salted black beans (also known as douchi, fermented black soybeans or Chinese fermented black beans) are used widely in Asian cooking, especially in black bean sauce. They are made from soybeans, which are fermented and then dried. They are available from Asian grocery stores and online food stockists.

Gelatine is a colourless, odourless substance made from collagen derived from animal by-products. We use leaf gelatine, which is sold at specialty food stores and delis. Gelatine leaves are available in different strengths, so instead of stating the number of leaves to use we've given gram measurements so you can adapt the recipes for the various types of leaf gelatine that are available.

Ice-cream stabiliser is sold in powdered form. It's a mixture of gum, starches, emulsifiers and proteins that helps improve the texture of ice cream and sorbets by suppressing crystal growth. It's available from specialty pastry suppliers and online stockists.

Liquid glucose is a sweet thick, clear syrup used in lots of desserts and jams. Because it prevents crystallising, it works really well to make ice creams, sauces and other sweet dishes silky smooth. It's available in the baking section of most supermarkets.

Masa flour (also known as masa harina or harina de maíz) is finely ground cornmeal used widely in South American and Mexican cooking for making corn tortillas. It's available from specialty food stores and delicatessens, and also from specialty online stockists.

Mezcal (mescal) is a Mexican spirit made from any agave plant. Tequila, which is a regional mezcal, is made from the blue agave plant only.

Mojama is salt-cured air-dried tuna from Spain that can be sliced, shaved and even grated over all kinds of dishes. Although it comes already dried, it can sometimes be a bit soft and fresh so we usually wrap ours in a clean cloth and leave it in the fridge for a week to dry out even more. It looks like a piece of wood and almost tastes like jamón. If you notice that it's white on the outside, that's just salt — scrape it off and it'll be absolutely fine. We love it, and grate loads over our fish fingers (page 4). You can buy it from quality food stores or online from specialty food shops.

Old Bay is a special herb and spice blend from Chesapeake Bay, Maryland. It's sold by McCormick & Company in the US and used to flavour crab, prawn (shrimp) and other seafood dishes. We get ours through a specialty food supplier.

Sodium nitrate is a type of salt widely used for preserving and curing food. It is sold in powder form and is usually 'pure', which means it needs to be mixed with salt before using. We use it in small quantities for our homemade sausages and cured meats to make them safe.

Tapioca maltodextrin is a modified starch used as a carrier for flavours and as a thickening agent. It's pretty much tasteless, and is sold in powder, flakes or little balls. We love using it to dehydrate ingredients and turn them into powder or dust. You don't have to do much to it at all, just mix it with other ingredients and it turns them into a fluffy powder, which turns back into something silky and light in your mouth when you eat it. Better quality maltodextrin gives lighter, better results.

Trimoline (also known as invert sugar syrup) is syrup made by heating and adding an acid (such as citric acid) to simple sugar syrup. Because it retains moisture, it's used in baked goods to make them nice and moist. We also like using it in ice creams because it prevents crystals from forming. It's available from specialty pastry suppliers and online stockists.

Type A culture is a starter made from specially selected bacteria. It's added to milk during the cheese-making process to help develop the flavour and texture of cheese. This type of culture is suitable for making many different types of cheese. It is available in sachets from online stockists. We use cheeselinks.com.au.

UHT (Ultra heat treated) milk is also known as 'long-life' milk. It is pasteurised and homogenised in the same way as fresh milk, but is then treated with a powerful heat that kills harmful bacteria and allows the milk to be stored (unopened) out of the fridge for a long period of time. It's available in most supermarkets.

Vegetarian rennet is used in cheese-making to help the milk set into solids. Historically, rennet has been made from enzymes found in the stomachs of animals such as sheep, cows and goats, but plant-based enzymes have become more common and are widely available online and in specialty food shops.

Xanthan gum is made from fermented cornflour (cornstarch) and is widely used as a thickener. It's gluten free and available from health food stores and some supermarkets.

If you can't find some of these dry goods and powdered ingredients in your area, one of our favourite Australian online specialty food stockists is The Food Depot, which is based in Melbourne: melbournefooddepot.com

INDEX

INDEX

INDEX

ACKNOWLEDGEMENTS

Where do we begin when it comes to thanking and acknowledging all the people who have made our story, and this book, possible? Both only exist because they are the sum of all their parts.

THE STORY
Friends & Family
A life of hospitality often means a great deal of sacrifice and understanding from your nearest and dearest. We thank our family and friends for all their love and limitless amounts of understanding. For all the lunches, dinners and parties we've missed because we were working; for all the times we feel like the only time we see you is when you come to see us at the restaurants; for always forgiving us for being late or not turning up at all. Mostly, however, for your endless support.

Our Restaurant Family (staff past & present)
We started with a small team made up mostly of family members. Over the years, the many members of staff that have come and gone have become like extended family members. Each and every one of them deserves a personal thanks, but there are too many to mention and in fear of missing someone, we're thanking you all. We hope you know who you are. The legacy of their contribution exists in the menus we continue to serve and the customers who keep coming back.

To our customers, who brave the queues, wait for tables and — best of all — keep coming back. Without your continued support and encouragement we wouldn't be able to open our doors. A special thanks to our regulars old and new, you've become part of our family.

Special Thanks
Joe: We dedicate this book to him. He's our business partner, brother and, above all, our dear friend! We owe you more than money could ever re-pay.

Sarah (from Elvis): Thanks to my wife, Sarah Doyle, whose support and hard work went above and beyond to make this book happen. You inspire me every day. I do it for you.

Rachael: It's fair to say that at the beginning we had little idea how to run a restaurant. We knew how to cook, but a restaurant is as much about the service as it is about the food. At the very beginning of Bodega, Sarah's sister Rachael kindly offered to help a few days a week to get the restaurant going, hire and train the staff, implement systems and make sure it all ran like a professional restaurant. Rachael was the only one amongst us with any real experience. Two days a week turned into six days a week, 12 hours a day, and over the past seven years we've operated, nothing has changed. Like Joe, Rachael is always in the background making sure the bills are paid and the garbage gets collected — all with little or no recognition. Thank you, Rachael. We couldn't do any of this without you.

Hilda & Adan: Elvis's folks are our secret weapons. Adan has taught us more than any other chef we've worked for, and to this day he works tirelessly alongside us each day, as does Elvis's mum, Hilda, who also bakes and cooks for the staff. We often think she's the reason they stick around.

Ana: Elvis's sister, who goes out and secretly sources cool ingredients for us to try. We often don't even know where she gets them.

THE BOOK
We can't imagine it's easy to work with people like us, who have such a clear vision of what they want and how they want it, but there's no way we could have made this book ourselves. The entire process has been a journey shared and enjoyed by the following phenomenally talented people and new-found friends:

Jane Lawson: Jane introduced us to the world of publishing, and she helped us believe that we had a story worth telling.

Sally Webb: We began this journey with Sally and she gave us the confidence and guidance to know this book was possible. We hope you are proud of where it has ended up.

Livia Caiazzo and Miriam Steenhauer: Both worked behind the scenes on this from the beginning. Thanks for being a bridge between us and Murdoch and for keeping all the moving parts moving.

Anson Smart: Anson is responsible for most of the incredible photos in this book, and they are all works of art in their own right. Anson was one of the very first photographers to shoot in Bodega when it opened. We loved his work then and still do.

David Morgan: The only stylist we have ever let touch our food. He understood our style and our vision and made our food look even better than we could have.

Sonia Greig: We think the readers should thank Sonia, because without her these recipes wouldn't work as well as they do.

Katie Bosher: Her meticulous editing eye and lightning-fast typing helped us get this book to you on time. She was always a pleasure to work with.

Andrew Quilty: Who has become our favourite in-house photographer as much for his talent as for the fact that we love hanging out with him. It was only fitting that his beautiful photos made it into this book.

Myffy Rigby: We are known for our cooking, not our literary abilities so we can't thank Myffy enough for writing this book with us. She gets us! Myffy knows what we want to say, but more importantly she knows how to say it the way we wish we could. There was never anyone else we would have had help tell our story.

Our Friends: Who helped bring our picnic chapter to life. When nature decided a perfect picnic might not be so perfect, Marc and Sue opened their beautiful home to us all. Our friends made this day (as they do so many days) perfect. We love them all, not because they have the best cars and the most enviable wardrobes, but because they are so kind and generous with their love and time.

Our Inspiring Contributors:
BT
David Chang
Alex Atala
Dan Auerbach
We are so honoured to have met and got to know these guys, and to have shared good times with them. We thank them for contributing to our book and giving us great stories to tell. You all inspire us.

And last, but not least, to the greatest artist we've had the pleasure of working with, *Michael Wholley.* We always knew he was the one to turn our story into a book because he takes every idea and makes it better. We always say it hardly seems fair that one man should have so much talent but we are eternally grateful that he does. Thank you, Michael, from the bottom of our hearts.

Thank you

To be continued ...

Published in 2013 by Murdoch Books, an imprint of Allen & Unwin.

Murdoch Books Australia
83 Alexander Street
Crows Nest NSW 2065
Phone: +61 (0) 2 8425 0100
Fax: +61 (0) 2 9906 2218
www.murdochbooks.com.au
info@murdochbooks.com.au

Murdoch Books UK
Erico House, 6th Floor
93–99 Upper Richmond Road
Putney, London SW15 2TG
Phone: +44 (0) 20 8785 5995
Fax: +44 (0) 20 8785 5985
www.murdochbooks.co.uk
info@murdochbooks.co.uk

For Corporate Orders & Custom Publishing contact
Noel Hammond, National Business Development Manager,
Murdoch Books Australia

Publisher: Sue Hines
Designer: Michael Wholley
Illustrations: Michael Wholley
Photographer: Anson Smart
Stylist: David Morgan
Food Editor: Sonia Greig
Editor: Katie Bosher
Design Manager: Miriam Steenhauer
Editorial Manager: Livia Caiazzo
Production Manager: Karen Small

Text © Elvis Abrahanowicz and Ben Milgate 2013
The moral rights of the authors have been asserted.
Narrative text: Myffy Rigby
Additional text: Katie Bosher
Design © Murdoch Books 2013
Photography © Anson Smart 2013
Additional photography provided by Andrew Quilty p v, p 142, Michael Wholley pp xvi, 5,14, 15, 24, 32, 33, 49,
Getty images p 191, Gabriele Stabile p 55.

The publisher would like to thank Carriageworks for the use of their buildings and Marc and Sue for opening their
home for the picnic shoot.

A cataloguing-in-publication entry is available from the catalogue of the National Library of Australia at www.nla.gov.au.

A catalogue record for this book is available from the British Library.

Colour reproduction by Splitting Image, Clayton, Victoria.

Printed by 1010 Printing International Ltd, China.

IMPORTANT: Those who might be at risk from the effects of salmonella poisoning (the elderly, pregnant women,
young children and those suffering from immune deficiency diseases) should consult their doctor with any concerns
about eating raw eggs.

MEASURES GUIDE: We have used 20 ml (4 teaspoon) tablespoon measures. If you are using a 15 ml (3 teaspoon)
tablespoon add an extra teaspoon of the ingredient for each tablespoon specified.